New Challenges
for Educational Research

OECD

ORGANISATION FOR ECONOMIC CO-OPERATION AND DEVELOPMENT

ORGANISATION FOR ECONOMIC CO-OPERATION AND DEVELOPMENT

Pursuant to Article 1 of the Convention signed in Paris on 14th December 1960, and which came into force on 30th September 1961, the Organisation for Economic Co-operation and Development (OECD) shall promote policies designed:

- to achieve the highest sustainable economic growth and employment and a rising standard of living in member countries, while maintaining financial stability, and thus to contribute to the development of the world economy;
- to contribute to sound economic expansion in member as well as non-member countries in the process of economic development; and
- to contribute to the expansion of world trade on a multilateral, non-discriminatory basis in accordance with international obligations.

The original member countries of the OECD are Austria, Belgium, Canada, Denmark, France, Germany, Greece, Iceland, Ireland, Italy, Luxembourg, the Netherlands, Norway, Portugal, Spain, Sweden, Switzerland, Turkey, the United Kingdom and the United States. The following countries became members subsequently through accession at the dates indicated hereafter: Japan (28th April 1964), Finland (28th January 1969), Australia (7th June 1971), New Zealand (29th May 1973), Mexico (18th May 1994), the Czech Republic (21st December 1995), Hungary (7th May 1996), Poland (22nd November 1996), Korea (12th December 1996) and the Slovak Republic (14th December 2000). The Commission of the European Communities takes part in the work of the OECD (Article 13 of the OECD Convention).

Publié en français sous le titre :
De nouveaux défis pour la recherche en éducation

Foreword

Complex societies and education systems require a sound knowledge base for practitioners and policy-makers. Educational R&D is contributing to new insights and a common knowledge base in education. An important issue is to which extent the national educational Research and Development (R&D) systems function as an effective means for creating, collating and distributing the knowledge on which practitioners and policy-makers can draw on. The Centre for Educational Research and Innovation (CERI) at the OECD has launched national reviews of educational R&D to address this issue.

This report explores, in particular, the educational R&D systems in two countries – England and New Zealand. OECD Review Teams have been assessing the effectiveness of the educational R&D systems in these two countries in developing and applying usable knowledge to improve the quality of educational practice and policy. The approach of the Review Teams is to analyse the national educational R&D system as a knowledge management system in which the basic purpose of educational R&D is to develop, organise, and disseminate information and knowledge that illuminates our long-range understanding of the fundamental processes of education. In the short term, it supports continuous improvement of the education system. These two reviews are presented in Chapters 2 and 4. The accompanying background reports prepared by the Department of Education and Skills, England and the Ministry of Education, New Zealand to support the work of the Review Teams are presented in Chapters 3 and 5. Chapter 1 highlights some of the key challenges and issues in educational R&D that OECD countries are facing.

The report shows that increasingly OECD countries are taking a number of innovative initiatives in order to improve the knowledge base in education for teachers and policy-makers through research. There are, however, still major knowledge and cultural changes needed in the practice of teachers, researchers and policy-makers in order to create a system-wide continuous improvement of the knowledge base for the education system. Teachers need to look beyond their schools for evidence and think rigorously about their practice. Policy-makers need to "value" and apply research evidence in the development of policy and implementation. Researchers must work more closely with teachers to improve the knowledge base on education practices.

The composition of the OECD Review Team for England's educational R&D systems was Professor Marshall Smith, Stanford University and the Hewlett

Foundation and former Under Secretary of the US Department of Education; Deputy Director General Karen Nossum Bie, Norwegian Ministry of Education and Research; and Director Stefan Wolter, Swiss Co-ordination Centre for Research in Education. The New Zealand review has been prepared by the Swedish Ambassador to Germany and former Swedish Minister of Education and Science, Carl Tham Professor Tom Schuller, Dean of Continuing Education, Birkbeck College, UK; and Professor Martin Carnoy, Stanford University, US. The two Background Reports for the reviews have been prepared by the Department of Education and Skills, England and the Ministry of Education, New Zealand respectively. Principal Administrator, Kurt Larsen from the OECD Secretariat, has been responsible for conceptualising and managing the project. This book is published on the responsibility of the Secretary-General of the OECD.

Table of Contents

Part II
New Zealand's Educational R&D System

NEW CHALLENGES FOR EDUCATIONAL RESEARCH – ISBN 92-64-10030-X – © OECD 2003

List of Boxes

List of Tables

List of Figures

ISBN 92-64-10030-X
New Challenges for Educational Research
© OECD 2003

Chapter 1

Key Issues in Educational Research and Development Systems in OECD Countries

Abstract. *A large part of the criticism of the educational R&D systems has been that much of the research has been of little relevance to practice and policy. OECD countries have taken policy initiatives to support the effectiveness of their educational R&D system to meet the increased demand for research and information about education. Some of the major initiatives are :*

1. Increased focus on use-inspired basic research.

2. Systematic accumulation and dissemination of knowledge.

3. Strengthening research capacity system-wide.

4. Improving the reform of education through a research-based continuous improvement strategy.

The CERI report entitled "Educational Research and Development – Trends, Issues and Challenges" from 1995 studied the means and ends of improving the knowledge base for educational practice and policy-making. It underscored both the importance of educational R&D in this process and the obvious need to improve its relevance and efficiency. It was concluded in the report that this largely depends on whether diverse interests can be aligned and better partnerships forged among the "three communities" – researchers, practitioners and policy-makers.

Some of the problems that were identified in the OECD 1995 report were that a great deal of the educational R&D was seen as fragmented, politicised, irrelevant, and too distant from practice (p. 22). Furthermore, the research was sometimes perceived as provincial and too little based on international experience (p. 24). Such a critique is still strong today. A recent report from 2001 prepared by Professor Antoine Prost for the French Ministers of Education and Research on the French educational R&D system concludes that the educational research is uncoordinated, rarely used, not evaluated systematically, and not sufficiently international (Prost, 2001).

This is not to say that educational researchers have not produced new insights, but they have, in general, been less successful in synthesising this knowledge for application and action by practitioners and policy-makers. This of course has to be put in the context that the resources for educational R&D are very limited compared with other major sectors of the economy. A rough estimate of the level of educational R&D as a percentage of total expenditure on education is on average less than 0.3 % in six countries for which data are available. This is a very small figure when education is compared with other knowledge sectors, for example, the health sector where between 5-10 % of the total health expenditure in public and private sectors are devoted to R&D.

The identification and debate about these problems in the educational R&D system have, in many cases, served a useful purpose in bringing about change in educational R&D. It has often provoked self-evaluation in the research community and stimulated some countries to make the research system more efficient and effective in contributing to the knowledge base for practice and policy-making.

Furthermore, two general trends increased the demand for more research and information about education in several OECD countries. First, governments increasingly are steering educational systems by goals and standards rather than governing by rules and regulations. This raises the need for more R&D information on the outcomes of education practices and policies both at regional, national and international levels. The wide use of the OECD's Programme on International Student Assessment (PISA) should be seen in this light. Second, several governments are promoting "evidence-based" policy making. The core of such an approach is that policy initiatives should, as far as possible, be underpinned by evidence and research. A good example of such an approach can be found in the US Bush Administration's first domestic initiative, the reauthorization of the Elementary and Secondary Education Act, entitled "No Child Left Behind." The Act mentions "scientific based research" 110 times. Scientific based research is thus intended to serve as a basis for several programs under this Act.

OECD countries have taken policy initiatives to support the effectiveness of their educational R&D system to meet this increased demand for research and information about education. Some of the major initiatives are mentioned under the following headings 1) balancing the research portfolio; 2) accumulation and dissemination of knowledge; 3) capacity building; and 4) supporting and improving the reform of education through a research-based continuous improvement strategy.

The overview does not cover all the initiatives taken by OECD countries to support their educational R&D system. This would be a very ambitious task. The policy initiatives mentioned are mainly from what is known from the reviews on educational R&D systems carried out in England and New Zealand (Chapters 2-4). Both the Department for Education and Skills in England and the Ministry of Education in New Zealand have recently increased their spending on education research projects and centres considerably. In spite of some policy and education system convergence in OECD countries, educational R&D is strongly anchored in national political and social contexts.

1.1. Balancing the research portfolio

A large part of the criticism of the educational R&D systems during the 1990's has been that much of the research has been of little relevance to practice and policy. As a reaction to criticism, several countries have taken initiatives to promote educational R&D which simultaneously addresses problems of practice and promises new knowledge. This kind of research has been called "use-inspired basic research" by Stokes who is arguing that many fundamental advances in science have been stimulated by applied problems (Stokes, 1997).

As mentioned in the OECD Review Team report of England's educational R&D system (Chapter 2), the government has changed the balance between pure basic research and pure applied research to emphasise use-inspired basic research through dedicated research centres and through the Economic and Social Research Council's Programme on Teaching and Learning. In New Zealand, the Ministry of Education's initiative to formulate strategic research priorities for educational R&D at the national level can also be seen as an initiative to strengthening the users' role in identifying research topics and generic discussions on educational research and knowledge management in national educational systems in the CERI Governing Board. Another approach, of which there are examples in the United States, is to support a small number of very ambitious research projects to look at a difficult problem of practice over a longer period.

The current American Administration is giving a higher priority to evidence-based education policies through, for example, the newly reauthorized Institute for Educational Science for what was the Office of Educational Research and Improvement. The reorganised Institute is going to spend a larger part of its research budget to randomised experimental research on education programmes and policies.

The US educational researcher, Robert E. Slavin, is arguing that rigorous experiments evaluating replicable programmes and practices are essential in building confidence in educational research among policymakers and educators (Slavin, 2002). He is welcoming the increased use of randomised experiments that transformed medicine, agriculture, and technology in the 20th century and are now beginning to effect educational policy and practice. Other educational researchers are more sceptical to which extent randomised experiments on education practices would be able to significantly improve the knowledge base in education practice and policy.

The jury is still out whether our knowledge about "what works" in educational practice can be significantly improved much in the same way as it has been the case in medicine, and consequently, whether it is possible to quickly improve the effectiveness of the education system. The human activity involved in teaching and learning is extraordinarily complex, and education deals with desired states rather than stable phenomena, and these are debatable and contestable.

Over the coming years, it is very likely that education policy-makers and educators increasingly will demand more research and information and that especially "use-inspired basic research" will be high in demand. A key issue is whether education researchers in general have strong incentives to carry out use-inspired basic research. Compared to other major sectors such as health and engineering where use-inspired basic research is heavily rewarded, the reward mechanisms in education sector have been less focused on such research.

It is argued in the Examiners' report on England (Chapter 2) that the Research Assessment Exercise (RAE) in England, which mainly rewards research in terms of international, academic excellence, to some extent conflicts with the demands to disseminate research in ways that might impact on policy and practice. Several initiatives have been taken to revise the criteria in the RAE to ensure that high quality, relevant and practical research will also be credited. For example, the criteria were revised to recognise curriculum, teaching and assessment material where justified by the underlying research and more users of research have become members in the panel that is assessing education research in the RAE.

Across OECD countries, the educational R&D effort is mainly concentrated on compulsory schooling and to some extent on early childhood education. There is less research on higher education and especially lifelong learning, as well as research on the interaction between policy and practice in different spheres, for example between education and the labour market, or between education and health. This is certainly the case in both England and New Zealand; however, new research programmes in higher education and lifelong learning have recently been launched in both countries.

1.2. Accumulation and dissemination of knowledge

The Review Team report on England's educational R&D system argues that successful management of research in education should set framework conditions and incentives to make research easily accessible, cumulative in nature and focused on usefulness. Existing knowledge should be a basis for any new investments in research in order to optimise the quality of ongoing research and increase the value added of new research. The development of new information technologies, including the Internet, have clearly widened the possibilities of making research easily accessible and cumulative in all scientific disciplines including education, not only nationally, but increasingly, also internationally.

The institutions that have responsibility for accumulation and dissemination of education research are often national based and focused mainly on national research programmes and results. These can be open databases on research programmes and projects, easy accessible journals for practitioners on research results, specialised libraries and research journals, etc.

Two interesting examples of recent established institutions with a primary focus on systematising and disseminating education research results are the "Evidence for Policy and Practice Information and Co-ordinating Centre" (EPPI-Centre) based in England and the What Works Clearinghouse (WWC) in the United States.

The prime role of the EPPI-Centre is to lend support for those wishing to undertake systematic reviews around what is known about a range of educational policy and practice issues. The systematic reviews aim at including a wide range of research perspectives and methodologies. There is some evidence that these methodological developments have begun to influence funders in their commissioning of research proposals. It is still too early to evaluate the impact of the systematic reviews under the auspices of the EPPI-Centre in influencing education policy and practice. In the OECD Review Team report on England (Chapter 2), the work of the EPPI-Centre is seen as the most important effort in England for accumulating knowledge on educational research and the Review Team has encouraged the Department for Education and Skills to support this work on a longer term basis.

The What Works Clearinghouse is a newly established project by the US Department of Education's Institute of Education Sciences, to provide educators, policymakers, and the public with a source of scientific evidence on what works in education. The Clearinghouse is a joint venture of the American Institutes for Research and the Campbell Collaboration, an international research group based at the University of Pennsylvania. It will aim at producing high quality summaries of research on the effects of educational interventions and approaches on students' outcomes; promoting the use of rigorous scientific methods in studies of educational effectiveness; promoting the use of rigorous research in education decision-making; and facilitating public and educator access to research-related resources. A set of standards being developed for WWC review activities has been released in November 2002 for public comment. The end product of the review process is the creation of WWC evidence reports that will be made available on the Internet.

It might be possible to establish a stronger collaboration on an international and comparative knowledge base on what works in education based on the experiences of the EPPI-Centre, the WWC and other initiatives. The Campbell Collaboration is such an attempt to "developing systematic reviews across countries" which includes areas like crime and justice, social welfare and education. The Campbell Collaboration is based on the same concept as the Cochrane Collaboration, which systematically collects reviews findings from randomised experiences in health care. The Cochrane Collaboration is a successful example of international research collaboration with a high impact on practice and policy in health care, and more than 15 Cochrane Centres have been established around the world.

1.3. Capacity building

The performance of the education systems to produce, disseminate and apply new knowledge depends on that all the "three communities" –

practitioners, policy-makers and researchers – having the capacity to do so. It is not enough to strengthen the capacity of the education research community to deliver high-level basic and applied research. If the capacity among practitioners and policy-makers to interact with the researchers and to apply this new knowledge into new practices and policies is not in place, then the continuous improvement of the education system will be slow. In a coherent strategy for improving the efficiency of the education system, it is therefore necessary to focus on capacity building of all the three communities.

In some OECD countries such as the UK, it is difficult to attract young talented researchers into education research. Furthermore, the average age of educational researchers is high in some OECD countries, which implies that many of them will retire in the coming years. Another generic issue is the lack of educational researchers who have competent skills, especially in quantitative methodologies. There is thus a critical need for new and experienced researchers with adequate training in both quantitative and qualitative methodologies. These issues can, and should to a large extent, be addressed by the academic community itself but in some cases it would need support from the education authorities.

The challenge of strengthening the involvement of practitioners in educational research and development is paramount. There are however several obstacles: first, the dominating concept in several circles and countries is of teaching and learning as an art, and the study and development of education as a separate scientific activity. Second, the average teacher has not received training nor developed competence in research methodologies. Third, teachers are often not trained to use research evidence in a systematic way. In Sweden, it is compulsory that teachers at all levels do a small piece of scientific research as part of their initial teacher training. However, this obligation is not widely applied across OECD countries.

Several countries have launched programmes and networks to encourage teachers to interact with researchers and to do "practitioner research" by themselves. In the UK, the Teachers Research Grant Scheme, Best Practice Research Scholarships, National Union of Teachers' Scholarships and the Networked Learning Communities promoted by the National College of School Leadership are all initiatives which aim at strengthening teachers' capacity to carry out research and to work professionally with academic researchers on research projects. In Sweden, a university reform has encouraged universities to work closer together with regional communities and more specifically schools of education with local school authorities and research projects.

Teachers' unions have increasingly shown interest in supporting teachers who carry out research and investigations to strengthen their knowledge base about teaching and learning. Educational research and development has a key role in enhancing the status of the teaching profession through developing teachers as an evidence-based profession.

Policy-makers in education have often not been trained in interpreting research results as part of their job. The political process is very complex in education. The idea of a knowledge base mainly consisting of simple linear relationships between certain policy actions and certain educational outcomes is generally a myth. Increasingly, OECD Ministries of Education are promoting their own internal research competence as well as improving their information and assessment systems designed to improve the overall functioning and transparency of the education system. In general this promotes policy-makers' capacity to engage with researchers and understand research evidence, and how to use it in their daily work.

There are no quick "solutions" when the aim is to improve the research capacities of not only researchers, but more system-wide, including practitioners and policy-makers involved with education. This is bound to be a long-term strategy where sustained effort is necessary.

1.4. Improving the reform of education through a research-based continuous improvement strategy

The key question is what action needs to be taken to increase the education system's capacity for the successful production, mediation and application of knowledge. OECD work on knowledge management in different sectors has shown that the rate, quality and success in knowledge creation, mediation and use are relatively low in education compared with the health and high-tech sectors (OECD, 2000). Part of the explanation can be related to the fact that teachers possess relatively little in terms of a common body of codified, explicit knowledge to underpin their work. Teachers' professional knowledge is thus personal rather than collective, and more tacit than explicit.

In the knowledge society, the capacity for each individual to learn throughout life is crucial. Teachers, especially at school level, therefore need to teach students to "learn how to learn". All this requires the production and application of new pedagogic knowledge on a huge scale and teachers have to be actively engaged in it through collaborative professional effort rather than by pure research. This new pedagogical knowledge on a large scale requires that teachers become more collaborative. Networking would be a key element in such an effort by using both internally and externally existing networks, strengthening them and using them more systematically. Information technology and the Internet could be useful tools in enhancing the network building. A system-wide knowledge management approach in schools where teachers continuously seek to improve their professional knowledge is most likely the most fruitful way forward (OECD, 2000).

Educational researchers can play an important role in such a system-wide approach to continuously improve the knowledge base in education. This would imply much tighter partnerships and collaborations between researchers and teachers, by which they engage in sustained dialogue to design, implement and evaluate R&D projects or researchers move into schools to work alongside teachers as R&D partners. Such a role for university-based, educational researchers contains:

- training and supporting practising teachers in research skills, including knowledge validation, to enable them to carry out more school-based research for knowledge creation;
- interpreting their partnership with teachers less often as occasions for transmitting academic or research knowledge to them and more often as opportunities to contribute to the integration and combination of different kinds of knowledge as an important ingredient of teacher-led knowledge creation;
- co-ordinating dispersed, school-based R&D programmes, from small-scale, preliminary knowledge creation in a consortium of two or three schools to large-scale, multi-site experiments, in order to create bodies of cumulative knowledge about effective pedagogic practices; and
- helping to disseminate the outcomes through networks of schools and teachers;
- making the study of the creation, dissemination and validation of knowledge in education a focus of university-led research (OECD, 2000).

Such school-based research and development would not replace basic research in universities and research institutes, but would be complementary and enrich it.

The review of England's educational R&D acknowledges that England has embarked simultaneously on a strategy of improving its education system and the capacity of its educational R&D system. It recognises that England potentially has an important opportunity to demonstrate how research may be applied to improve education practice and policy at the national level. All OECD countries are working towards improving their education systems; however, these reforms are not always based on systematic reviews and papers on best practices which are an important beginning for a sustained and rigorous effort of understanding and improving implementation processes.

There are still major knowledge and cultural changes needed in the practice of teachers, researchers and policy-makers in order to create a system-wide continuous improvement of the knowledge base for the education system.

Teachers need to look beyond their schools for evidence and think rigorously about their practice. Policy-makers need to "value" and apply research evidence in their development of policy and implementation. Researchers must work more closely with teachers to continuously improve the knowledge base on education practices and "what works" (use-inspired basic research). These cultural and knowledge changes are beginning to take place in a number of OECD countries.

Bibliography

OECD (1995), *Educational Research and Development – Trends Issues and Challenges*, Paris.

OECD (2000), *Knowledge Management in Learning Societies*, Paris.

Prost, A. (2001), "Pour un programme stratégique de recherche en éducation", Rapport remis à MM. les ministres de l'Éducation nationale et de la Recherche par le Groupe de travail constitué par M. Antoine Prost, ministère de l'Éducation nationale, Paris.

Slavin, Robert E. (2002), "Evidence-Based Education Policies: Transforming Educational Practice and Research", *Educational Researcher*, Vol. 31, No. 7, pp. 15-21.

Stokes (1997), *Pasteur's Quadrant – Basic Science and Technological Innovation*, Brookings Press, Washington, DC.

PART I

England's Educational R&D System

ISBN 92-64-10030-X
New Challenges for Educational Research
© OECD 2003

PART I

Chapter 2

OECD Review of England's Educational R&D System
Examiner's Report October 2002

Abstract. This chapter presents the OECD review of England's educational R&D system. The purpose of these reviews is to assess to which extent the educational R&D system within a country is functioning as an effective means for creating, collating and distributing the knowledge on which practitioners and policy can draw. The general assessment of England's educational R&D system is positive. The directions taken in the many initiatives to improve the knowledge management of England's educational system are convincing. Some of the ambitions behind continuous improvement of the knowledge base for England's education system will, however, demand major knowledge and cultural changes in the practice of teachers, researchers and policy-makers.

2.1. Overview

Purpose

This is the second OECD review of a Member country's educational R&D policy. The report has two goals. It reviews the policy of a specific country, England, and reaches some conclusions concerning that country. It also contributes to an emerging understanding of important educational R&D policy issues common to many OECD nations.

Our statement of purpose for the review is taken from the report of the Department for Education and Skills (DfES), "Research and Development in England: Background Report Prepared for the OECD Review" (DfES, 2002), which states: "The purpose is to review the extent to which the educational R&D system within a country is functioning as an effective means for creating, collating and distributing the knowledge on which practitioners and policy can draw." Thus, the report may be viewed as an evaluation of the effectiveness of England's educational R&D system in developing and applying usable knowledge to improve the quality of educational practice and policy. To carry out the evaluation, we examined national policies and agendas for educational research and development, as well as the organisation and resources of the educational R&D system.

Approach and methodology

The review team brings a variety of perspectives and experiences regarding educational R&D and national policies. Each of the reviewers has been actively involved in OECD activities for decades and all have served in positions of substantial responsibility in their nations' governments.

The review team spent five days in England interviewing a wide variety of people in government and in groups actively involved in educational research and practice (see Appendix 2.1 for a complete list). Four days were spent in London in intensive meetings. The fifth was spent in Newcastle where we visited the School of Education and some very impressive classrooms at St. Thomas More School and Longbenton Community College. In preparing for the visit, we relied heavily on the Background Report and on other materials prepared by a wide variety of constituent groups.

The complexity and breadth of the educational R&D system in England combined with the short period of time available for the study forced us to bring a great deal of humility to our task. Our review is a broad sweep through what we have identified as critical issues. It has not been the purpose of our review to focus on the quality of educational R&D in England, but to assess the government's R&D policies in the field of education. We cannot therefore generalise about specific areas of study, about the quality of R&D or even about research as a factor in the discussion of specific policies. We debated models for structuring our thoughts, formed impressions, tested ideas as we progressed through the week, brought our own experiences to organise the information we received, and have gone through a process of writing and rewriting our impressions and conclusions.

Our interviews and the DfES Background Report concentrated on pre-collegiate education. Our focus has thus been almost exclusively on pre-collegiate education practice and policy. As a result, the review provides very limited analysis of higher and adult education. However, throughout the report we suggest that certain generic issues, such as accumulating knowledge, dissemination of research and research capacity are also relevant to tertiary and adult education.

Overall impressions

We left England impressed in a number of dimensions. The quantity and quality of attention being paid to educational R&D by the government and to its potential contribution to the quality of policy and practice are remarkable, especially when contrasted with the other nations with which we are familiar. In terms of quantity, we were impressed by the breadth and scope of new efforts to improve the quality and relevance of R&D. We should remark, however, that the investment, while substantial in comparison with that of some other nations, pales when compared with the level of investment in other knowledge industries.

Regarding the quality of attention to educational R&D, we found, among the people we interviewed, a striking level of understanding of research and of the government's attempts to improve the quality and utility of the R&D system. We also found a high degree of sophistication in the capacity of British social science to provide definitive evidence, as well as a refreshing lack of ideology in the discussions of research. Most of the interviewees seemed to understand that the improvement of education is a long-term process and that effective research can help steer this work in productive directions.

We found strong support for efforts to improve the quality and utility of educational R&D and an interest in complementing the government's efforts with efforts from organisations such as the British Education Research Association (BERA) and the National Foundation for Educational Research (NFER) in the independent sector. There is clear evidence of interest in sustaining the push to improve and rationalise research and to evaluate the overall effort. We must note, however, that there is some resistance to the government's plans among constituents and producers of research. This resistance is considered in further in this chapter.

Organisation of the report

The report has eight parts. This introductory part and the following two establish the context for our discussion. Section 2.2 reviews the current context of educational R&D in England and its recent history and concludes with some comparisons with educational R&D in other OECD countries. Section 2.3 introduces a model of an effective educational R&D system to guide our consideration of practice in England.

The remaining five sections contain our analyses and conclusions about current R&D efforts. In Section 2.4, we begin with an assessment of the quality and usefulness of current educational research and some suggestions for improvement. Section 2.5 examines issues of accumulating and disseminating knowledge, and Section 2.6 considers efforts to build R&D capacity, especially human capital. Section 2.7 examines ways in which research might support England's educational reforms and proposes a set of strategies that might be followed. Section 2.8 brings together our conclusions and summarises our recommendations.

2.2. Context of the OECD review

This section describes England's current educational R&D system. We start with a short description of the expenditures for educational R&D, examine the challenges to educational R&D in the recent past, and conclude with a consideration of recent changes resulting from efforts by the DfES and the research community to respond to the criticisms of the 1990s.

Current expenditures on education R&D in England

The Background Report (DfES, 2002) and the R&D Funding Sub-group Report from the National Educational Research Forum (NERF, 2001b) set out current expenditures on educational R&D. Four sets of figures stand out:

- A recent NERF estimate indicates total expenditures of approximately GBP 70-75 million a year. This amounts to less than 0.5% of the annual total expenditure on education and is far less than the average spent on R&D in the business sector or other knowledge-dependent organisations. Comparisons with other countries are difficult, but OECD (1995) provides some indicators that may be used for comparison. The level of educational R&D as a percentage of total expenditure on education is on average less than 0.3% in six OECD countries for which data are available (Australia, Canada, Finland, Ireland, the Netherlands, Sweden). US expenditures on educational R&D are significantly larger in monetary terms but are probably somewhat less in terms of percentage of total expenditures on education. It is important to note that such figures do not include funded research addressing issues relevant to education carried out in other discipline-based departments, such as studies of "how children learn", "brain development" and "organisational research studies".

- A large share of educational R&D funds come from government spending through the Higher Education Funding Council for England (HEFCE) (60%); the Economic and Social Research Council (ESRC) (5%); and other federal agencies and local government (14%). Charities account for approximately 7% and the balance is made up of income from the European Union (EU) and other international projects, industry and other sources, including a wide range of private-sector educational and training organisations. The lack of strong participation by the private sector in funding educational research creates special responsibilities for government. Although professional organisations may help, the responsibilities of ensuring quality, relevance and transparency will inevitably rest heavily on the backs of the people and organisations that make the financial allocation decisions. Indeed the heaviest responsibilities are borne by HEFCE, as illustrated by the fact that 60% of educational R&D funding is provided by the Council, while the Council's funding across scientific fields averages only 33% of the total R&D funding in those fields.

- By far the largest single source of government funds for research, the HEFCE, administers from 2002-03 some GPB 940 million dedicated to research. For educational R&D the figure is approximately GBP 40 million, almost all of which goes to universities to distribute to their departments of education. Universities are awarded the resources on the basis of a Research Assessment Exercise (RAE) carried out by a subject panel of academics and users that takes place every fourth or fifth year. The last review took place in 2001 and will inform funding decisions from 2002-03. The RAE rates departments on the basis of the quality of their published research and consequently there is a heavy reliance on publications in peer-reviewed journals. Universities have a great deal of flexibility in choosing how to spend the resources they receive from HEFCE *e.g.* they can provide extra resources for a subject they are keen to develop, or they may extract what amounts to a tax for overhead prior to allocating the funds to university departments.

- The NERF Sub-group Report estimates that 90% of educational R&D is carried out in university departments of education. While at least 100 separate institutions conduct education research, 80% of the funding from government, Research Councils and charities goes to 22 university departments or schools of education.

Two general conclusions stand out. One is that funding for educational R&D in England is small when education is compared with other knowledge-based sectors but probably not compared with other countries. The second is that resources for educational R&D are concentrated in university departments of education.

Challenges to educational R&D in England in the recent past

Over the past 20 years, the status of educational R&D in England, as determined by the government, has reached both a low and a high. Prior to the 1980s, much research, in particular action research, was promoted by organisations such as the Schools' Council and the Assessment Performance Unit. The low occurred in the 1980s during an era of educational reform that culminated in the adoption of a national curriculum. At the time, it was considered that educational R&D was unnecessary – the reformers believed that they already knew what they had to do to improve the quality of education. The formula was a national curriculum with clear standards, aligned assessments, reduction of regulations for schools, and accountability for results. In implementing these policies, the reformers expected the system to improve continuously, using assessment/accountability as a feedback mechanism to correct failures. Educational R&D in general received little government attention, and few resources were provided for research or evaluation addressing issues related to the implementation of the reforms.

By the middle of the 1990s, views had changed somewhat. Government officials found that implementation of the reforms had been more complex than expected, particularly in the area of classroom instruction. In 1995, the Teacher Training Agency (TTA) initiated an effort to characterise teaching as a research- or evidence-informed profession. In 1996, the TTA invited David Hargreaves to give their annual lecture. In his talk, "Teaching as a Research-based Profession: Possibilities and Prospects" (Hargreaves, 1996), Hargreaves' message was clear. He compared educational research with medical research and found educational research deficient in important dimensions: it was non-cumulative, not useful for improving schools and generally lacking in quality.

This view was not new, but the lecture was widely circulated and triggered a rash of writings, generally concurring with Hargreaves' conclusions, in scholarly and other settings (Edwards, 2000; Tooley and Darby, 1998; Hillage *et al.*, 1998). Tooley and Darby analysed the quality of published research. The Hillage *et al.* report, commissioned by the Department for Education and Employment (DfEE), analysed the funding and usefulness of educational research and was quite influential, Hillage *et al.* looked at how the system works and what impact it has. It concluded that the connections among research, policy and practice were weak; that research was too supplier-driven; that an emphasis on short-term evaluation, at the expense of exploration and development, led research to follow rather than lead policy; that studies examining practice were small-scale and unable to generate findings that could be generalised; that research findings were disseminated *ad hoc*; and that policy-makers and practitioners lacked the capacity to use research when it was available. This sweeping indictment set the stage for several policy changes.

The nature of R&D in England

Some of these reviews traced the "inadequacy" of research to the process of funding research (through HEFCE). The distribution of funds to a small number of university education departments was seen as reinforcing small-scale basic research projects carried out by independent researchers on topics that are more appropriate for publication in refereed, high-quality journals than for addressing pressing problems of practice or policy. Some critics even saw the incentive system based on RAE as almost ensuring that knowledge deriving from the research would not be usable.

In response, of course, the process was defended as ensuring that funds went to well-trained researchers who, to receive funds and later publish their findings, had to undergo rigorous peer review. Moreover, some of the funds went to strengthen fields such as history and philosophy, where it is more difficult to imagine research that is directly related to practice or policy. Finally, HEFCE policy and procedures were defended as protecting "blue sky" research, here understood as theoretical research with little obvious or immediate practical application for education but which might not be funded by a government that wanted only immediately useful R&D. "Blue sky" research may also be understood to mean an investigation that challenges the status quo or does not relate to current policy, and on this definition, the HEFCE distribution system may be less efficient.

The challenge is to see how to balance "blue sky" (research with little practical application) with research that thoughtfully and rigorously addresses contemporary education problems. The research funded by HEFCE, which makes up 60% of the total research outlays, may or may not address practical issues. Indeed, part of the problem is that there is no way of knowing what HEFCE money to universities is used for. However, the clear impression that we received was that the incentives that drive the allocation of HEFCE funds operate to push HECFE research away from having a practical bent. Fundamentally, the criticisms of the English educational R&D system in the late 1990s focused on the lack of usefulness of the research for informing policy development and practice. Figure 2.1, taken from *Pasteur's Quadrant* (Stokes, 1997), focuses on the problem of usefulness and addresses the issue of research that is both basic (fundamental) and useful in terms of two dimensions, "quest for fundamental understanding" and "considerations of use".

Figure 2.1.   **Pasteur's Quadrant**

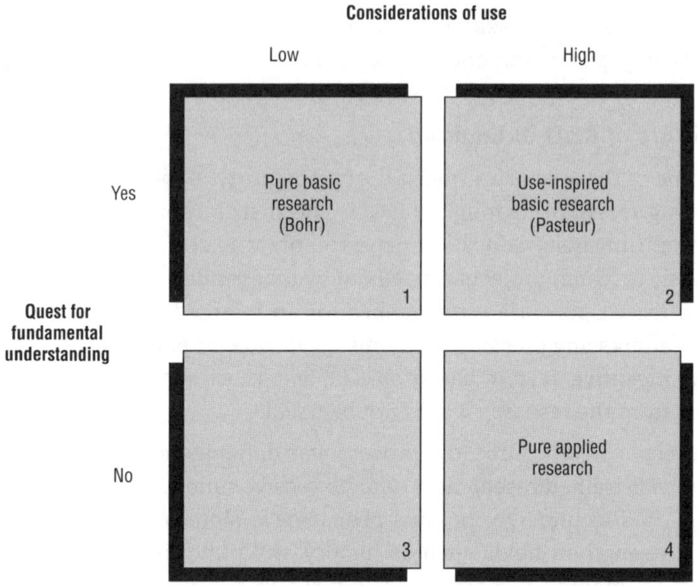

Source: Stokes, 1997.

Stokes argues that basic research can be both "pure" and "use-inspired" and that many fundamental advances in science have been stimulated by applied problems. The fact that research is applied does not mean that it is also not basic. Quadrant 2, "use-inspired basic research", called "Pasteur's Quadrant", reflects his core argument, and the relative absence of educational research of this sort in England prior to the late 1990s appears to represent the central criticisms of Hargreaves and Hillage et al.

DfES's response to the critics

In response to the criticisms, the DfES moved quickly to put into place an aggressive strategy to reform research policy and move it towards the kind of research that would fit in Pasteur's Quadrant. The Department's task, however, was and is difficult, because it has little influence over most government resources for educational R&D, which are mainly controlled by HEFCE. Thus, the Department would use its resources to fund research to balance HEFCE funding, to influence scholars' incentives to carry out research that would generate useful knowledge and to address issues related to the accumulation and dissemination of such knowledge.

Given such constraints, DfES has generated an impressive record over the past few years. Some of its accomplishments are to have:

- Almost doubled DfES's research budget since 1997. Although the base was small (GBP 5-10 million), the direction and slope are positive.

- Established in September 1999, the National Education Research Forum to provide strategic direction for educational research. NERF has established a Funder's Forum to explore possibilities for greater collaboration between funders. The Forum proposes to establish an Education Priorities Group to develop a methodology and criteria for identifying priorities for educational R&D. Furthermore, the Forum will establish an Education Observatory to examine current and emerging developments as well as medium- and longer-term trends likely to shape the future. The Observatory will also develop a method for setting research priorities.

- Created and funded dedicated research centres for co-ordinated, systematic and "use-inspired basic research" focused on "wider benefits of schooling", the "economics of education", "information and communication technology", and "adult literacy and numeracy".

- Provided partial support for launching two major longitudinal studies, one on 14-21 year olds and the other on a cohort of 20 000 babies born between July 2000 and June 2001.

- Provided funding for England's participation in international studies that provide benchmarks for assessing national progress.

- Worked with HEFCE on the RAE to attempt to leverage funds to be more focused on useful research by influencing the criteria for judging research, and the balance of types (to include users) of reviewers and by working with journal editors.

- Worked with teachers and teacher unions on a variety of efforts to include information about problems of practice in research agendas. This has included setting up with the Teacher Training Agency a National Teacher Research Panel of teachers who advise on research issues.

- Addressed problems of accumulation of research information by setting up, supporting and accelerating the work of the Evidence for Policy and Practice Information and Co-ordinating (EPPI) Centre for carrying out systematic reviews in education.

- Leveraged funds from HEFCE money administered by ESRC to fund a coherent research programme focused on teaching and learning and to organise a network of researchers to focus on these issues.

Education reform in England

The change in government policy, from almost ignoring educational R&D to embarking on a concerted effort to improve it, is reflected in other efforts throughout the government and a vigorous strategy to better implement educational reforms. Professor Michael Barber, the Prime Minister's Chief Advisor on Delivery, Cabinet Office, describes the changes in a paper delivered in Zurich in April 2002 (Barber, 2002). He emphasises that a primary goal of the current administration is better delivery of public services. Continuously improving the implementation of educational services, using better information about the effects and the needs of customers, is a critical component of this policy. Essential in this effort is greater access to effective and useful information gathered through research and evaluation and the strengthening of capacity in the delivery systems.

Barber captures the past two decades of pre-collegiate education policy and the current direction of policy in the model in Figure 2.2.

In brief, he argues that in the early years of the national curriculum reforms, the Conservative government moved from a system of low challenge and low support to a system of high challenge and low support. The Conservative government's answer to the "stagnation" of the system was new standards, new tests and accountability, but it invested insufficiently in the resources needed to support the move towards higher standards. According to Barber,

Figure 2.2.   **Education policy**

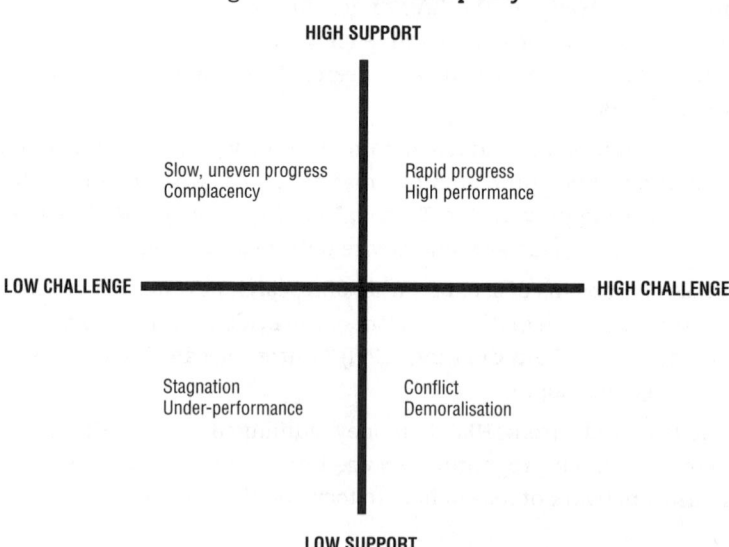

Source: Barber, 2002.

"Nor was enough done to address the social circumstances which, particularly in declining industrial areas and large cities, made the job of educators daily more difficult. The result was some improvement but also conflict and demoralisation".

The response to this analysis by the Labour government in 1997 was not to reduce the challenge but to increase support, creating a policy approach described by Barber as "high challenge, high support". Part of the increase in support was to promote and increase the quality and usefulness of educational R&D.

Effectiveness of educational R&D in other OECD countries

Research evidence is used to support the improvement and reform of education in many OECD countries. In the United States, for example, the Clinton administration initiated standards-based reforms and pursued a policy of improving the implementation of government programmes. The Bush administration has continued the reforms while also advocating "evidence-based" policy making, especially in education. In France, a report on educational R&D from Professor Antoine Prost to the Ministers of Education and Research (Prost, 2001) drew conclusions very similar to those of Hillage et al. Educational R&D in France was characterised as unco-ordinated, of limited use and often improperly assessed in terms of quality. This report led in late 2001 to several initiatives by the French Ministry of Education to strengthen the co-ordination of providers of educational R&D, train a new generation of education researchers and establish better dialogue between researchers and all actors in the education system. In Denmark, New Zealand, Scotland, Switzerland and Wales, similar discussions and initiatives are taking place. The fact that other nations are addressing such problems reinforces the importance of England's effort. It is important to note, however, that in England and other nations, the resources allocated to educational R&D are desperately small compared to the amounts allocated to R&D in other sectors. It is ironic that the core societal institution for improving understanding and developing human capital receives one of the lowest allocations of funds for informing and advancing the field.

2.3. Conceptualisations of an educational R&D system

The national educational R&D system as a knowledge management system

To structure our consideration of the England's educational R&D system, we decided to approach it as a knowledge management problem (OECD, 2000; 2001). In this context, the basic purpose of educational R&D is to develop, organise and disseminate information (knowledge) that illuminates our long-range understanding of fundamental processes of education. In the short term, it supports continuous improvement of the education system. The review team used two models to describe educational R&D and its place in the overall field of R&D.

We also sketched out four dimensions of an educational R&D system. Together with the models, the four dimensions provide the structure for our analysis of England's system.

Basic and applied research

One model, shown in Figure 2.3, is a wheel, with basic research in the centre and spokes representing areas of applied research. Basic research is typically defined as focusing on understanding fundamental laws and relationships and building theory, and is typically unconnected to immediate use. Applied research tackles understanding and solving practical problems. In the United States, the National Science Foundation would be located in the middle of the wheel while applied research at the National Institutes of Health, the Office of Naval Research and the Office of Education Research and Improvement would be located on one or another of the spokes. In England, the same kinds of distinctions are made by HEFCE, by the Research Councils, which fund university-based basic and applied research, and by various departments of the government that fund applied research.

Two observations are relevant. The first is that the arrows suggest that knowledge flows in both directions. This reminds us that applied educational research benefits from a wide variety of disciplinary research that is not labelled as educational research, such as studies of learning in psychology and neurobiology, organisation theory in sociology and the use of incentives in

Figure 2.3.   **Basic and applied research**

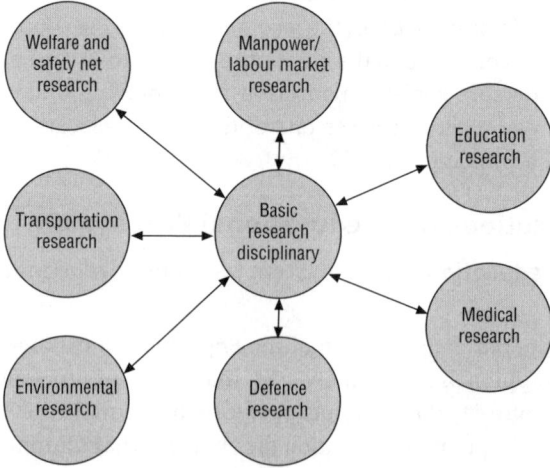

economics. The second observation is that in HEFCE's distribution of research funds for education, it is assumed that education is a discipline, and the funds are expected to be used for the development of theory and fundamental laws and relationships, (research in quadrant 1) rather than for developing a basic of understanding and solving problems of practice (quadrant 2). Although institutions determine the actual content of the research funded by HEFCE the examiners reached a conclusion that the process and incentives embodied in the HEFCE have a powerful influence that tilts research toward quadrant 1.

Interrelationships among basic research, applied research, interpretation and dissemination and policy and practice

Figure 2.4 adds the categories of "interpretation and dissemination" and "policy and practice" to the R&D model. The figure suggests a somewhat linear process from basic to applied research to interpretation and dissemination, and finally to practice and policy within the national context. This linear model has been criticised as too simplistic. The double-headed arrows indicate the potential for feedback. While a complete model would be far more complicated, this one indicates the important feedback loop between applied R&D, on the one hand, and policy and practice, on the other. It also suggests that the process of interpretation (including synthesis) is crucial for taking applied research into the realms of policy and practice.

Figure 2.4.   **Traditional R&D model in a national educational system**

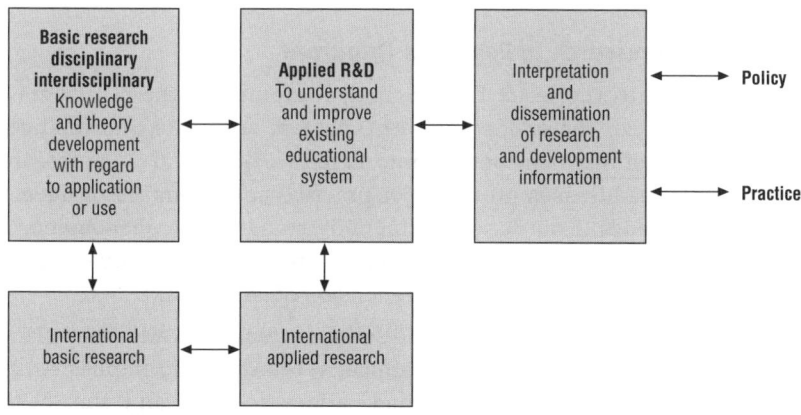

Dimensions for organising our thoughts about the R&D system

Finally, as the review team considered the English system of educational R&D, we used some general criteria to structure our thinking. We did not attempt to apply these criteria to specific examples but used them in thinking about the nature of the R&D system. Four dimensions stood out: balance in the nature of the research; quality and availability; capacity; and the relationship of the research to school improvement and reform. These dimensions capture the basic ideas and suggestions that emerged from the variety of interviews that we carried out and are strongly represented in the Background Document (see Chapter 3) and in the various documents that we perused during our week in England.

In essence, we are asking a series of four questions: does the system produce applied as well as basic research? Is the knowledge developed by the system of high quality and is it available to potential users? Does the system have enough resources, including human resources, to meet the needs of its users effectively? Are products of the system useful for improving the effectiveness of schools? These questions, and the related four dimensions, form the organising concepts for the following four parts of the report.

2.4. A balanced research portfolio

The efforts by DfES and others to reform the educational R&D system have been ambitious when compared with efforts in other OECD countries. Have they been ambitious enough to meet the standard set by Barber (2002) in the title of his talk, "From Good to Great?" Probably not. Throughout the rest of the report, we look at various aspects of the R&D system and offer ideas about how to focus better on understanding, supporting and improving the English educational system.

Need for more research in Pasteur's Quadrant

We start with the issue that seemed to dominate the criticisms of the 1990s. How can the educational R&D system stimulate and finance a greater amount of research that fits into Pasteur's Quadrant? Such research simultaneously addresses problems of practice and promises to develop knowledge that adds to our fundamental understanding of a phenomenon. A simple example is the question of the role of the size and complexity of a person's vocabulary and her/his comprehension of written text.

The current government has made serious attempts to alter the balance between pure basic research and pure applied research and to emphasise use-inspired basic research. It has also made efforts to focus on issues of the quality and impact of research. The development of dedicated research centres and the ESRC's Programme on Teaching and Learning are two good examples. Perhaps the most important event has been the establishment of NERF (to bring together researchers and users of research and to help establish a research agenda that is politically independent). Independent and respected voices of this kind are crucial to the quality of the discussion about research. This is a very important body for improving the level of credibility necessary to change national policies for educational research. Once this is done, the long-term role of NERF is not clear; it might help to monitor the quality and usefulness of educational research.

HEFCE has also made some small changes in its funding allocation priorities. In this area, users, teachers and other practitioners now have a greater voice in judgements about the quality of educational R&D and in the distribution of HEFCE funding. Finally, the DfES's discussions with journal editors about honouring research stemming from practice and the selection of reviewers are a promising move.

Taken together, these and other efforts appear to have influenced the picture of the independent university researcher working alone on problems that are essentially unrelated to improvement of the current education system. But, this tradition is strong in English and other European universities and in the United States, and the faculty of Schools of Education often try to emulate their colleagues in the discipline faculties. Pressures to produce this kind of work are powerful and the incentives to change are weak. The culture of the university in this regard is reinforced by the way in which HEFCE funding is allocated, and by the prestigious journals in education, which often attempt to emulate discipline-based journals. These conditions are deeply entrenched in university culture and reinforced by professional norms. It may be possible to make changes to the way that HEFCE resources are distributed and to alter substantially some of the priorities of the journals, but it seems unlikely that it will be possible to change the basic structure of the university.

One conclusion is that even if HEFCE funding were completely allocated according to criteria that reinforce practice-focused basic research, the norms and traditions of the university would still operate as a constraint on the nature and usefulness of the research. This is not to say that the research coming out of the universities is not important and useful – it is. However, the university is not conducive enough to large-scale problem-oriented work involving people working in teams, often in the field and at a considerable distance from the universities.

It is too early to judge the quality and results of the research centres or the Teaching and Learning Programme and its associated network, but our sense is that these efforts are in the right direction. The nation's portfolio could benefit from greater investments in long-term team-based and problem-based R&D.

We have learned from experience in education and other areas that research carried out at centres can vary greatly in quality and coherence. However, centres focused on significant educational problems, with a clear mission and goals, strong theories of action and effective mechanisms of quality control, can produce very important and relevant research, as well as ensure dissemination. The most persuasive examples from the United States are the Learning Research and Development Center (LRDC) at the University of Pittsburgh, the Consortium for Policy Research in Education (CPRE) at the University of Pennsylvania, the Reading Center at the University of Illinois, the Wisconsin Center for Education Research (WCER) at the University of Wisconsin at Madison, and the Center for Research on Educational Standards and Testing (CREST) at UCLA. These centres represent a range of organisational structures. For example, CPRE is, in part, a virtual organisation, owing to its partnerships with Stanford, Harvard, the University of Michigan and the University of Wisconsin. Each of these institutions has a member on the centre's governing board, as well as separate sub-grants for projects suited to each institution's strength. CREST has co-directors from two universities almost 1 000 miles apart, while the Wisconsin centre houses a large variety of projects.

As DfES works with its first round of centres, it would do well to develop careful evaluations and to ensure that each centre reflects upon its work. Refunding of centres is also an important decision and should entail a rigorous independent assessment. We also think it would be useful to begin to plan for a new round of centres to augment the existing set. NERF and the research community would likely play an important role as the missions for new centres are considered.

A second important strategy is to adequately fund a small number of very ambitious, but carefully designed, studies to look closely at a difficult problem of practice. In the United States at the University of Michigan, Professors Steve Rodenbush, Deborah Ball and David Cohen are carrying out such a study with some funding from the federal government although private foundations are supplying most of the funding. They are conducting a seven- to nine-year study of how teachers can teach mathematics effectively in very low-income schools using a sample of close to 100 schools. Among other products, the study is creating some powerful instruments for assessing the quality of instruction in mathematics. We might imagine similar studies carried out in England. For example, one study might examine ways of improving professional development by focusing on effective use of formative assessments in elementary or middle schools.

A third strategy is to create networks of researchers and practitioners around core problems of practice. Such networks can take a variety of forms, including a virtual structure using the Internet, satellite conferencing for formal or informal meetings.

2.5. Accumulating and disseminating knowledge

To make the best use of educational R&D in policy making and teaching practice, three problem areas have to be considered. First, existing research has to be inventoried and disseminated adequately. Barriers to accessing existing research hinder the impact that knowledge can have on policy making. Second, research itself suffers if new research does not systematically take account of and build upon the findings of earlier studies. To optimise the quality of ongoing research and increase the value added of new research, existing knowledge should be a basis for any new investment in research. A specific aspect of the non-cumulative nature of research in education is the fact that international research is often not taken into account. Third, to make the best use of the limited resources available for research, the focus should be sufficiently user-oriented and not just "supplier-driven". Successful management of research in education should therefore set framework conditions and incentives to make research easily accessible, cumulative in nature and focused on usefulness.

A variety of initiatives have been implemented in the past to accumulate knowledge about research on education in a better way. For cumulative effect, it is important for information to be disseminated through all appropriate channels to make it as soon as available as possible. The following sections examine the most important developments.

Documentation and dissemination

Several institutions in England currently inventory research and disseminate research results to a broad public. These institutions can be divided into several groups according to their core mission and their specific method of inventorying or disseminating research. Traditional institutions, including universities and research institutions specialised in research on education, such as the National Foundation for Educational Research (NFER), all document and disseminate research results. Most of this activity is restricted to each institution's research, and dissemination is mainly oriented towards specific user groups.

Among traditional institutions, specialised libraries also play an important role. The most important in this case is the British Education Index (BEI) based at the University of Leeds, which provides not only bibliographical information about research but also other resources for researchers. The Index office is increasingly diversifying its information services and is actively experimenting with customised delivery. Still, the traditional organisations mostly serve specialists and professionals, as access to the information remains difficult. Popularisation of research findings and transmission to a larger audience is currently supported by parts of the electronic and printed media.

Although these institutions sometimes invest heavily in documentation and dissemination of research, some new institutions have also been created to serve this purpose. The new institutions complement existing organisations and primarily fill the gaps in coverage of the traditional ones. The most prominent new institutions are Current Educational Research in the United Kingdom (CERUK) and Centre for the Use of Research and Evidence in Education (CUREE).

The DfES, the NFER and the EPPI Centre jointly developed CERUK. Researchers are the prime users of this freely accessible, Internet-based resource. The database holds information on current educational research projects undertaken in the United Kingdom, and the researchers themselves supply all the information in the database. Quality is therefore not a consideration for inclusion.

CUREE is commissioned by the DfES to identify and summarise published research findings with particular users in mind (not specifically researchers), as well as to provide quality assurance. The summaries are longer than the information provided by CERUK and are written by specialists in web based communication whereas one of the aims of CERUK is complete coverage of current research in the United Kingdom. CUREE restricts itself to a small number of high-quality studies featured in research journals that relate to issues identified as priorities by research users. The digests serve as standards for access to quality research and are also intended to encourage web oriented drafting by researchers. Information available from CUREE is disseminated on the Web site of the DfES.

Pedagogical and Educational Research Information Network for Europe (PERINE), a project funded by the European Commission, is a new project that attempts to combine existing sources of information on research in education on an international platform. So far, PERINE has eight participating countries; it is headed jointly by the BEI and the German Institute for International Educational Research (DIPF). PERINE's main users will be researchers interested in knowing more about foreign research or conducting comparative analyses. The accumulation of "other national" knowledge (the purpose of PERINE) on one platform should also contribute to the accumulation of "national" knowledge within England. The establishment of PERINE is also a reaction to an increase in comparative research in education (infrastructure follows demand) and shows the need to examine national R&D policies in a more international framework.

Initiatives to make research more cumulative

Considering the efforts made on different levels and by different stakeholders to improve and enlarge the documentation of research undertaken in the United Kingdom, we can assume that the biggest obstacles to cumulative research are being removed. However, we should not expect that these efforts alone guarantee that researchers and policy-makers will take previous research into account when starting new research or developing new policy strategies. A good dissemination policy may also be an incentive to work

38

cumulatively, as it raises the awareness of existing work among users and therefore the expectations attached to new research.

As lowering the barriers to information will not be sufficient to change research behaviour on all fronts, DfES has taken action to put in place more powerful direct and indirect incentives that will have the desirable side effect of increasing cumulative research. Among the direct measures are systematic reviews of research in particular fields. The most notable indirect measures are changes in the funding mechanisms of research and changes in DfES's management of research and statistics.

An important component of this effort is the EPPI Centre and the thematic reviews it undertakes to address education problems. Once a review in a certain field (or on a specific question) is completed, the review sets the basis on which new research will have to build. The higher the quality and the greater the dissemination of such reviews, the lower the probability of a researcher engaging in a new study without taking into account current knowledge, standards and methods.

Funding mechanisms can play a central role in setting incentives for cumulative research. In this respect, the creation of the "Funders' Forum" may contribute to raising the quality of research. Co-ordination among funders can help to avoid double funding and perhaps spark competition among funders that will raise the pressure for higher quality and less redundant studies.

Funding strategies may also lead to more cumulative research by concentrating research in fewer institutions. The RAE mechanism of funding clearly leads to a clustering and concentration of research in fewer universities. As a consequence, research may become more cumulative, as it will be less difficult to build on existing or ongoing research if most of the research is done in a small number of institutions than if it is scattered among a large number. The counter-argument is that there are often few experts in the same area in a single institution, and this may reinforce the traditional view of the independent researcher working on problems that are essentially unrelated to the current education system. The RAE may therefore encourage more cumulative research, not necessarily the kind of research that is most needed, the use-inspired basic research of Pasteur's Quadrant.

DfES's management of research also plays a central role in many other respects. One of its most powerful instruments is the "dedicated" research centre, in which research in a specific field is promoted in a single entity. Here, the argument is the same as for the concentration of research in fewer institutions owing to a change in funding strategy. At the same time, the Department has seen the need to increase "in-house" knowledge in order to contract and supervise outside research more efficiently. Increased "in-house" knowledge is one key to improving the overall quality of research. Informed users will ask for higher quality and more focused research and will therefore be more selective in contracting researchers (Hillage *et al.*, 1998). To this end, "the Centre for Management and Policy Studies in the Cabinet Office and the Civil Service College have developed a general programme for senior civil servants and ministers designed to promote a better understanding of evidence" (DfES, 2002, p. 8).

DfES' management of statistical sources on education also plays an important role. Small-scale, non-repetitive investigations produce data sets that do not serve the purpose of cumulative research. Concentration on the production of freely accessible, large-scale data collection with the guidance of researchers is one positive step. Longitudinal surveys (the DfES currently supports ten longitudinal studies), cohort studies ("The Millennium Cohort" led by ESRC) and participation in international cross-country studies will further increase the move towards more cumulative research.

As many researchers use longitudinal or cross-country data, this generates a culture of comparing analysis, methods and results and building upon others' knowledge.

Research between supply and demand

Even where research is well-documented and cumulative, it may not focus on policy or users. Cumulative research may extend and improve what researchers have done in the past, but may not be in areas of high interest or priority for users. In such cases, we speak of "supplier-driven" research.

Although a refocusing of research on user interests is observable, we argue that use-inspired basic research should be more strongly rewarded. However, users have to understand better how research works and accept the inherent long-term nature of research.

Reforms and proposed measures to improve the educational R&D system

The policies observed in the areas of inventory/documentation, dissemination, improvement of quality and refocusing of research all represent positive changes in the landscape of research on education in England. Measures to improve the situation further should therefore focus primarily on sustaining these reforms, and in some cases, enlarging their scope. A prerequisite to the accumulation and dissemination of know-how is a freely accessible research database. However, access to free research literature is not guaranteed everywhere, and initiatives like the "Open Archives Initiative" (*www.openarchives.org*) would deserve closer attention.

As a result, while recognising the difficulties that still need to be addressed, the review team emphasises the value of the EPPI Centre. Building up the methodologies for scientific reviews, carrying out the reviews and exploiting the results for future research are the most important efforts currently needed for accumulating knowledge on educational research. To this end, the EPPI Centre should be supported on a long-term basis, if evaluation of its activities demonstrates that the centre is producing high-quality, effective work. In addition, making the EPPI activities broadly international in scope (perhaps by increasing collaboration with the Campbell Collaboration) could further increase the gain policy-makers and the research community may expect from the EPPI Centre. If similar centres could be created in other countries and similar reviews conducted, the gain in knowledge would be greater and some economies of scale could be expected in terms of methodology.

The role of the "dedicated" research centre is also very important, as it acts as an incubator for user-relevant research. To maintain quality in these centres, the DfES should give them a high degree of academic freedom, while keeping open the potential for competition among research institutions. The entry of alternative institutions should be considered periodically to ensure that current centres are under competitive pressure to create high-quality work. The DfES will have the difficult task of maintaining a balance between concentration of research and competition between institutions.

In addition to efforts to improve the usability and quality of basic research, several programmes use practitioners (teachers and students) as researchers. To increase the capacity of practitioners to engage in research, DfES has created a support system via fellowships, grants, scholarships and special networks. It is evident that if research is to have an impact on practice in schools and classrooms, practitioners with experience in research are needed, but the link back to research is less evident. The efforts made in programmes using teachers as researchers should also generate information that can be fed back into more traditional forms of research. For this to happen, the management and overall design of practitioner research should be strengthened, and an investment should be made to synthesise these research findings and place them in a systematic and theoretical framework. Dissemination of research results (e.g. through teacher networks on the Web) should also be improved, with the condition that there should be some kind of quality control. The creation of a "mini" EPPI for practitioner research might be considered. The criteria for selection and retention of research results would probably be different from the current EPPI methodology and would need to be tailored to practitioner research. This would benefit interested users, university researchers and, above all, new practitioners who might engage in research and could build upon previous work.

Finally, in the long term, good quality research that generates cumulative knowledge relies on the formation of a group of well-trained researchers. Section 2.6 will examine this process by analysing capacity-building in English educational R&D.

2.6. Capacity building

Increased focus on capacity building

Capacity building among researchers, teachers and policy-makers is becoming an important issue in the overall management of England's education system. Several recent initiatives and reports have focused on capacity building. A major capacity-building initiative is currently under way as part of the ESRC Teaching and Learning Research Programme. One of the capacity building initiative's goals is to widen the methodological approaches and encourage high-quality management of complex projects in educational R&D. Furthermore, NERF has established a sub-group on building research capacity, which defines research capacity as "the resources – material, human and intellectual – that are available in the education system for doing and for using research, together with the (more or less effective) ways in which those resources are brought to bear". We agree with this broad understanding of "capacity building" and suggest that it might be more helpful to think about "research capacities". For instance, the capacity to produce scholarly research is somewhat different from practitioners' capacity to produce and use research to inform their practice, which is also different from policy-makers' capacity to use research. This suggests that it is unlikely that a few simple measures would quickly increase the capacity of the educational R&D system.

An important reason for the new focus on capacity building is the criticism made by researchers, policy-makers and other users of educational research that the educational R&D system lacks the capacity to produce high-quality research relevant to users. The present government's emphasis on evidence-based policy also contributes to the need for good and relevant research. Many different national initiatives have been taken at different levels to improve research capacity. These initiatives address the key areas relevant to human capacity in the system: education researchers; users, including teachers; and government officials. Initiatives pertaining to each of these groups are discussed in this section, which ends with a set of conclusions.

Capacity building and education researchers

We heard several times during our interviews about the difficult recruitment situation for talented young researchers and about the high average age (54 years old) of education researchers. Two-thirds of the current academic education research community are over 50 years old (DfES, 2002). Because of the age distribution, many researchers and teaching staff will retire in the coming years. Furthermore, education, like other academic disciplines, is facing increasing competition for talent from other knowledge sectors of the economy.

A survey of the present recruitment situation in universities and colleges in the United Kingdom points to the fact that several academic fields, including education, face particular difficulties for recruiting academic staff. The report emphasises that the difficulties may intensify because of problems resulting from the current age profile of the workforce and the government's plans to expand higher education (HEFCE *et al.*, 2001).

Trained personnel at the postgraduate and postdoctoral level are essential to maintain research capacity in education. While pointing to the value of the more traditional route through classroom and other relevant experience into educational research, the NERF sub-group report on research funding (2001b, p. 6), expresses concern that not enough young researchers are being attracted directly into educational research. According to the report, appropriate career path development is inadequate, although initiatives are being taken by ESRC and HEFCE to improve the situation.

We recommend a detailed analysis of the overall recruitment situation in educational R&D. Although several reports over recent years have addressed the issue of "shortage" of highly qualified education researchers, none has come to a final conclusion concerning whether recruitment is a serious problem. For example, the latest paper to NERF on capacity building mentions that "there does seem to be some evidence that lack of capacity may be a problem in the development of the national strategy [for R&D]" (Dyson and Desforges, 2002). A study currently under way at the University of Cardiff on capacity building could provide a useful background for such an analysis.

What is certain is the enormous need for new staff in education in universities and colleges over the coming years. This will also be an opportunity for renewal of staff in the field of educational research. It provides a chance to bring young researchers (with stronger methodological training) and researchers with different disciplinary backgrounds into educational research. Stipends for young Ph.D. students to spend time abroad or participate in international research projects would also contribute to capacity building and strengthen the internationalisation of educational research.

One of the critical needs for new and experienced researchers is adequate training in quantitative and qualitatitive methodologies. We heard over and over about the lack of competent quantitative researchers. Based on our review, much educational research is small-scale and qualitative in orientation. Comparatively little research is carried out using advanced quantitative methods that allow for large-scale and replicable research. While there are increasing opportunities to investigate large data sets, there are too few researchers with the necessary skills and experience. Furthermore, a combination of qualitative and quantitative methods is often required for research on complex issues in education, but too few researchers are sufficiently trained and experienced in both (DfES, 2002, p. 18). More training in well-designed experimental evaluation and systematic reviewing is needed. All this points to the need not only for strong methodological training for young researchers but also for professional development in these areas for some established education researchers.

Some initiatives aim to improve the methodological training of education researchers. The ESRC is funding different types of initiatives that will benefit the field of education. For example, Ph.D. programmes now require initial master's level research training, and all funded students in master's programmes undertake training in a wide range of methodological and other research skills. Courses at the master's level are being funded for government researchers, and student research opportunities are specifically linked to capacity building in the field of large-scale surveys. The range of ESRC training courses is being increased and some Ph.D. funding is being allocated to research centres for quantitative approaches. A National Co-ordinating Centre for quantitative design is being established, and a new GBP 4 million Research Methods Programme has been announced. Generally, work involving large and complex data sets is being encouraged by the government (Gorard, 2002). Other positive developments are the fellowships initiated by the British Educational Research Association (BERA) for part-time Ph.D. study for practising teachers, local education authority staff and others, linked to the ESRC Teaching and Learning Programme and the possibility for Ph.D. students to be afffiliated with the dedicated research centres.

As already mentioned, the ESRC Teaching and Learning Programme has capacity building in educational R&D as one of its objectives, and a special Capacity Building Network has been established at the Cardiff University School of Social Sciences to promote building capacity in research skills. Initiatives are varied and include training events, workshops and publications. These efforts are directed at both established researchers and students on different training programmes (master, Ph.D.).

We believe that these initiatives will contribute to the improvement of the research capacity of education researchers. To secure expertise among future generations of researchers, however, the review team recommends including courses in research methodology as an obligatory part of Ph.D. training, thus building on the training received at the master's level. In this regard, the initiative of the NFER together with the University of London/ Institute of Education, King's College London and the University of Oxford to establish an alternative route to the Ph.D. by way of an internship on a research project, deserves support.

Capacity building for evidence-based practice by teachers

As early as 1995, the Teacher Training Agency started to develop strategies to promote teaching as a research-informed profession (DfES, 2002, p. 7). To improve teacher involvement in research, a number of scholarships, networks and schemes have been established by the DfES and by different organisations, such as the TTA Teacher Research Grant Scheme, the National Union of Teachers' Scholarships, the BERA fellowships, the DfES Best Practice Research Scholarships (BPRS) programme and the TTA school-based research consortia. The TTA and DfES set up the National Teacher Research Panel that has had a significant input on research commissioning, steering and dissemination. Initiatives such as these support teachers' continuing professional development. Teachers are able to carry out small-scale, classroom-based research projects supported by a mentor/researcher from a higher education institution or a local education authority. The goal of these projects is to undertake enquiries into classroom practice, carry out investigations into teaching strategies and to share learning with colleagues. The National College of School Leadership is also promoting practitioner research through networked learning communities that enhance the professional development of teachers, including teachers' use of and involvement in research and evidence-informed practice is emphasised in management courses for teachers.

Programmes promoting capacity building in research for teachers are important and should be further developed. Quality control, good design and good guidance by experienced researchers are prerequisites. Local universities' involvement in a mentor role in such programmes would help in this regard. Teachers are usually pressed for time, and special efforts have to be made to facilitate research-based practice in schools. To initiate and sustain the development of schools as research-aware and research-using organisations, school management needs to be supportive and teachers need to be given a leading role in producing and using educational research in the school. A critical mass of teachers needs to be involved. Extra resources and adequate management of the development process are essential.

We saw impressive examples of TTA-supported networking in schools in Newcastle that are involved in small-scale research/investigations in co-operation with a local university department. The goal of these projects is to improve teaching methods and student learning.

Teacher involvement in research and the interpretation of research results also requires competence in research methodology and statistics. Scholarships and bursaries for teachers should offer such training as part of continuing education. It is important to train the new generation of teachers to use research in their practice and teacher trainees should receive such training in their pre-service education programme. We have understood that this is not an obligatory part of initial teacher training, but that some departments of education have introduced such training as part of their programme. The fact that teacher training often is located within university departments of education should provide good opportunities for teacher trainees to participate in research projects and in lectures on research methodology, thereby strengthening new teachers' competence in research management and methodology.

Capacity building in government

Since 1997, government departments in England have been involved in a modernisation process which has prompted the use of evidence-based policy. Special initiatives have been taken to promote better understanding of evidence and how it should be used, notably by establishing the Centre for Management and Policy Studies in the Cabinet Office (DfES, 2002, p. 8).

Hillage *et al.* (1998) point to the absence of time and intermediary support to help ensure access to research results for policy-makers and practitioners. As we have seen, the DfES has increased its budget for commissioning research outside the Department, as well as its internal research competence. This is improving the Department's capacity to engage with researchers, commission research and become a better and more critical user of research.

Capacity is co-ordinated across government agencies working on educational research by a research liaison group established to ensure better co-ordination of research programmes and greater consistency in commissioning and quality control procedures. Also, organisations independent of government attend the liaison group's meetings once a year, thus widening possibilities for better co-ordination.

A "culture" of evidence-based policy development is also built up in government departments because the Treasury Department, in its allocation of resources for new policy initiatives, often demands evidence that the proposed initiative will be able to achieve the specified policy goals.

In our talks with research officers and senior civil servants in the DfES, we received the impression that more emphasis is now placed on the use of research evidence in designing new policy initiatives and making policy decisions. That is not to say, however, that every new initiative or decision is based on research evidence.

Conclusions

The government has launched an impressive number of initiatives to increase research capacity among researchers, practitioners and policy-makers. We agree with the directions and goals of the initiatives. A key question is whether these initiatives are not somewhat disconnected and therefore have only limited impact on education policy and practice, as mentioned in the latest paper to NERF on building research capacity (Dyson and Desforges, 2002).

It is too early to offer a definitive answer to that question. More time is needed to evaluate these initiatives, and we are well aware that there are no "quick fixes" when the aim is to improve the research capacities not only of researchers, but also system-wide, including practitioners and policy-makers involved with education. It is our general impression that the average teacher at the average school is largely unaware of the "teaching as a research-based profession" initiatives. At some point, the DfES will have to decide whether the Department and others should continue to offer a small number of teacher research grants or take more system-wide measures, such as rewriting teacher training standards or reconsidering teachers' conditions of employment and advancement. Such reflections would be crucial for support for educational reform through the research-based, continuous improvement strategy that is the focus of Section 2.7 of this report.

2.7. Supporting and improving the reform of education through a research-based continuous improvement strategy

Over the past five years, England has embarked on an ambitious agenda to implement the national curriculum reforms of the late 1980s by focusing on using research to develop goals and incentives for the education system, as well ensuring that implementation is coherent and even creative.

In effect, the government has established a "theory of action" to guide its attempts to see England's educational system progress from "good to great". Fundamental to its goals is the development and implementation of a system of continuous improvement of education practice. Central components of its policies are "detailed teaching programmes based on best practice", good assessment data and clear targets, access to and use of best practice information, quality professional development, and effective intervention in the neediest schools. Each of these components should draw on research data.

This is a crucial and extraordinary challenge. Governments rarely spend much time thinking about implementation. They even more rarely announce that they intend to spend the resources necessary to understand how to improve implementation continuously.

Policy implementation with feedback loops

Figure 2.5 displays a model of policy implementation with R&D feedback loops. It describes relationships among policy, implementation/practice and research/evaluation. We are attempting to capture the sense of a strategy for the continuous improvement of implementation. In reality, of course, there are arrows from politics to implementation and evaluation as well as to policy development. But for the purpose of focusing attention on current efforts to move towards a "high challenge, high support" system, this model provides a basic understanding of feedback loops.

The government's simultaneous focus on evidence-based reform and improvement means that each of the components as well as the overall system of continuous improvement should draw on carefully amassed and organised research data. The review team believes that this presents a very important opportunity to demonstrate how research may be used to improve the quality of practice in an entire nation.

This work requires special attention to a variety of areas through research and development. For example, England has the opportunity not only to put high-quality assessments into practice for both summative and formative purposes but also to integrate both types of assessment. Formative assessments, in concert with examples of student work, would be a powerful means of guiding practice and informing parents, teachers and students about student and teacher success. At the same time, best practice strategies should be used to improve practice, based on the needs identified through analyses of formative assessments and student work. A second area for careful study would be the assessment of different strategies for devolving authority. What factors should influence the balance between top-down and bottom-up authority and responsibility? If we value devolution and believe it enhances performance, why do we abolish it when schools under-perform?

Systematic reviews and papers on best practice are important beginnings for the type of sustained and vigorous effort at understanding and improving implementation processes that we have in mind. The effort will be most important at two points: where students are most in need of special attention; and the point of interaction between teacher and student. At the heart of any improvement effort will be the development of a systematic way to improve the quality of teaching continuously, particularly in low-income and under-performing schools.

We would like to emphasise two possible important starting points for this work. One is the teacher as researcher project mentioned in Section 2.5, which we believe to be an excellent approach for encouraging teachers to think rigorously about their practice. The second is the strategy of formative assessment, which shows extraordinary results according to the systematic review of Black and Wiliam (1998). If these results withstand the scrutiny of careful review, the strategy of formative assessment could be used as the cornerstone of a process of continuous improvement of instruction across the nation. Significant implementation steps in this direction are already underway. All secondary schools in the nation have received materials, including video lessons, on the use of formative assessments. But, this is just a start. We can imagine a careful and well-funded body of R&D that embeds in the curriculum high-quality formative assessments (developed by teachers and researchers working together) and systematically seeks the most effective ways to administer and use this information to improve the quality of teaching. If the results lead from small studies to large-scale implementation, even at only the 75% level of effectiveness found by Black and Wiliam, the gains would be very substantial – in the neighbourhood of improvement of three-quarters to a full grade level.

England has an opportunity to improve the quality and productivity of its educational system substantially. The opportunity has been created by the existence of a challenging and relatively young national curriculum and a government that understands the need to provide opportunity in order to have "fair" accountability. The first step is a commitment to using R&D to improve implementation of the education reforms at all levels of the education system: classroom, school, district and country. We believe England has taken this step. Should England be vigorous and successful in its efforts, it will set a standard for the rest of the world. A substantial part of the opportunity rests on the careful implementation of well-researched strategies for improving the quality of instruction in the schools. England has made a serious start in the right direction. It must continue to invest in thoughtful and user-oriented research, which offers new ideas and approaches and suggests ways of improving existing practice.

Figure 2.5. **Implementing policy**

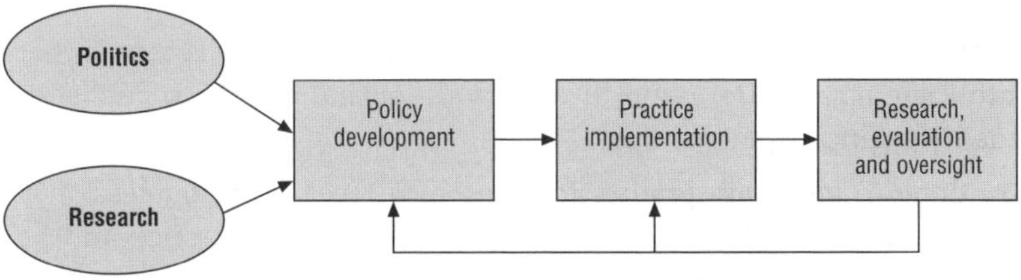

2.8. Conclusions and summary of recommendations

Our general assessment of England's educational R&D system is positive. Compared to other countries, there is remarkable support, both in quantitative and qualitative terms, of educational R&D and its potential contribution to the improvement of practice and policy within education. The directions taken in the many initiatives to improve the knowledge management of England's education system are convincing.

Whether the commitments, ambitions and initiatives are enough to move the education system from "good to great" is, however, in question. Some of the ambitions behind continuous improvement of the knowledge base for England's education system will demand major knowledge and cultural changes in the practice of teachers, researchers and policy-makers. Teachers need to look beyond their schools for evidence and think rigorously about their practice. Policy-makers need to "value" and apply research evidence in policy development and implementation. Researchers must accept that the results of the traditional individual university researcher working on a self-defined, small-scale research project is unlikely to influence practice and policy in education. These cultural changes are beginning to take place but are not occurring system-wide. We would like to suggest some recommendations that might help accelerate the necessary changes.

Our specific recommendations fall under five main headings 1) changing the portfolio of research; 2) the role of NERF; 3) accumulating knowledge; 4) capacity building; and 5) system-wide improvement of the education system through research.

Changing the research portfolio

We recommend creating a portfolio of research, in which more research would simultaneously address issues of practice or policy and issues of fundamental knowledge – that is, the research which falls into Pasteur's Quadrant (see Figure 2.1). We believe that, if carefully carried out, three steps would ensure a strong and well-balanced research portfolio that would usefully serve to support England's educational system:

- Ensure that NERF plays an active and productive role in developing research directions that illuminate issues of practice and policy.

- Continue to work with HEFCE's RAE to reward university research that fits into Pasteur's Quadrant and to work with journal editors to publish high-quality examples of such work.

- Continue to give high priority to using new research resources for large-scale research endeavours that focus on issues of practice and policy through the development of research centres, large-scale research projects and networks of researchers and practitioners that focus on understanding problems of policy and practice.

Continue the role of NERF

We recommend that NERF should continue to have a strong advisory role in improving the overall educational R&D system. NERF plays the important role of bringing independent and respected researchers and practitioners together to help establish a research agenda that is unconstrained by governmental politics. Furthermore, it is a crucial body for gaining credibility for changes in the direction of national policy on educational research.

NERF is a somewhat vulnerable body. It has almost no resources and no direct decision-making competencies and depends very much on the enthusiasm of its members and their contributions. This has worked well until now, as members are strongly committed to improve educational R&D in England. How can the positive momentum of the Forum be sustained? It might be worth reflecting on the role and composition of NERF in the longer term. The process for selecting members should be more transparent.

Increase the accumulation of knowledge

We acknowledge that many important initiatives have been taken to improve R&D in the area of documentation, improvement of quality and refocusing of educational research. We therefore recommend that the main focus should be on sustaining these initiatives and in some cases enlarging their scope. In this context, we place high priority on the work of the EPPI Centre. It should be mandated on a long-term basis, if an evaluation of its activities shows the organisation to be effective. Additionally, expanding EPPI activities internationally would increase the benefits researchers and policy-makers can expect from the Centre. Furthermore, the creation of some "mini" EPPI for practitioners' research might be considered.

We support the role of the new "dedicated" research centres, as they act as incubators for user-relevant research topics. To maintain the quality of these centres, and to inspire their creativity, the DfES should give them a high degree of academic freedom while keeping open the possibility of competition among research institutions, which would also involve all current centres bidding competitively for their continuation. The entry of alternative institutions should be considered periodically to keep the current centres under competitive pressure and ensure quality. These centres are in a strong position to ensure that the knowledge they produce is cumulative and stronger links should be made between the research centres, the EPPI centre and the National Educational Research Forum.

Increase research capacity

We recognise the impressive number of initiatives undertaken to increase research capacities among researchers, practitioners and policy-makers. We agree with the directions and goals behind these initiatives. There are no "quick fixes" when the aim is to improve the research capacities not only of researchers, but also system-wide. Programmes promoting capacity building in research for teachers are important and should be further developed, both through pre-service and in-service teacher training aligned on the goals of improvement initiatives.

Given the high average age of education researchers, it will be necessary to recruit a large number of new researchers in education over the coming years. This provides an opportunity to bring young researchers from different disciplines with an improved training background into educational R&D. There are some indications that it is difficult to recruit young talented researchers for educational R&D. We therefore recommend carrying out a detailed analysis of the overall recruitment situation in educational R&D. More specifically, we recommend that high quality training programmes in research methods become an obligatory part of Ph.D. training.

System-wide improvement of the education system through research

England is embarking simultaneously on a strategy of improving its education system and improving the capacity of its education R&D system. Its goal, as reported by Barber in conversation with the examiners, is to create, in effect, a process of "continuous improvement" at all levels of the education system: the classroom, the school, the district and the nation. We applaud this goal and urge that it be given a very high priority by the administration. We believe that this is a very important opportunity to demonstrate how research may be applied to improve education quality and practice in an entire country. It will be very interesting to follow these efforts, which will be most important where the students are most in need of special attention, particularly in low-income and under-performing schools.

Bibliography

Barber, M. (2002), "From Good to Great: Large-scale Education Reform in England, Futures of Education", Arbeit, Bildung und Beruf Conference, Zurich, Cabinet Office, London.

Black, P. and D. Wiliam (1998), *Inside the Black Box: Raising Standards through Classroom Assessment* King's College, London.

DfES (2002), "Research and Development in England – Background Report Prepared for the OECD Review", Department for Education and Skills, London.

Dyson, A and C. Desforges (2002), "Building Research Capacity: Some Possible Lines of Action", a discussion paper for the National Education Research Forum. Available at: *www.nerf-uk.org*

Edwards, A. (2002), "Responsible Research: Ways of Being a Researcher", *British Educational Research Journal*, Vol. 28, No. 2, pp. 157-168.

Edwards, T. (2000), "Some Reasonable Expectations of Educational Research", UCET Research Paper No. 2, Universities Council for the Education for Teachers, London.

Gorard, S. (2002), "Introduction to the ESRC TLRP Research Capacity Building Network", *Building Research Capacity*, Issue 1, Cardiff University.

Hargreaves, D. (1996), "Teaching as a Research-Based Profession: Possibilities and Prospects", The Teacher Training Agency Annual Lecture 1996.

HEFCE (2000), *Funding Higher Education in England: How the HEFCE Allocates Its Funds*. Guide.

HEFCE *et al.* (2001), Recruitment and Retention of Staff in UK Higher Education.

Hillage, J., R. Pearson, A. Anderson and P. Tamkin (1998), *Excellence in Research on Schools*, DfEE, London.

NERF (2001a), "A Research and Development Strategy for Education: Developing Quality and Diversity", National Educational Research Forum.

NERF (2001b), "Research Funding: Sub-group Report", National Education Research Forum.

NRC (2002), *Scientific Research in Education*, National Academy Press, Washington, DC.

OECD (1995), *Educational Research and Development – Trends Issues and Challenges*, Paris.

OECD (1996), *Knowledge Bases for Educational Policies*, Paris.

OECD (2000), *Knowledge Management in Learning Societies*, Paris.

OECD (2001), "Educational Research and Development Policy in New Zealand", Examiner's Report, Paris.

Prost, A. (2001), "Pour un programme stratégique de recherche en éducation", Rapport remis à MM. les ministres de l'Éducation nationale et de la Recherche par le Groupe de travail constitué par M. Antoine Prost, ministère de l'Éducation nationale, Paris.

Stokes (1997), *Pasteur's Quadrant – Basic Science and Technological Innovation*, Brookings Press, Washington, DC.

Tooley, J. and D. Darby (1998), "Educational Research – A Critique. A Survey of Published Educational Research", OFSTED (Office for Standards in Education), United Kingdom.

APPENDIX 2.1

Interviewed Persons

Professor Richard Andrews	University of York Department of Educational Studies/Universities Council for the Education of Teachers
Parin Bahl	Associate Director Strategic Education Services Capita
John Bangs	National Union of Teachers
Professor Michael Barber	The Prime Minister's Chief Adviser on Delivery Cabinet Office
Lorna Bertrand	Senior Executive Officer Assessment Department for Education and Skills
Audrey Brown	Divisional Manager Analytical Services Department for Education and Skills
David Budge	Deputy Editor (and research editor) Times Educational Supplement
Professor John Bynner	Centre for Wider Benefits of Learning (Institute of Education/Birkbeck College)
Peter Clark	Department for Education and Skills
Dave Clarke	Research Coordinator Longbenton Community College
Jim Cockburn	Principal Longbenton Community College
Professor Frank Coffield	University of Newcastle Department of Education
Dr. Gavan Conlon	Centre for the Economics of Education London School of Economics Institute for Education/Institute for Fiscal Studies

Philippa Cordingley	Centre for the Use of Research and Evidence in Education
Professor Charles Desforges	Previously Director of ESRC Teaching and Learning Research Programme
Anne Diack	Research Manager BBC Factual and Learning
Sue Duncan	Director of Policy Studies Centre for Management and Policy Studies, Cabinet Office
John Dunford	General Secretary Secondary Heads Association
Professor Alan Dyson	University of Newcastle Department of Education
Professor Anne Edwards	British Educational Research Association
Sir Brian Fender	Funders' Forum and former Chief Executive of HEFCE
Rhondda Garraway	Lecturer in pre-service training of FE teachers University of Greenwich
Nigel Gee	Senior Research Officer Analytical Services Department for Education and Skills
Professor Stephen Gorard	University of Cardiff Building Research Capacity Initiative, ESRC
Dr. David Gough	EPPI Centre
Gary Grubb	Teaching and Learning Research Programme, ESRC
Professor David Hargreaves	Advisor to Secretary of State for Education Former Professor at Cambridge University
Professor Seamus Hegarty	Director National Foundation for Educational Research
Carolyn Holcroft	Continuing Professional Development Department for Education and Skills
Professor David Hopkins	Head of the Standards and Effectiveness Unit Department for Education and Skills

Rob Hull	Director (Qualifications and Young People) Department for Education and Skills
Dr. Mary James	Cambridge University Teaching and Learning Research Programme, ESRC
Paul Johnson	Chief Economist Department for Education and Skills
Tim Key	Head of Research Office for Standards in Education Department for Education and Skills
Pat Leon	Times Higher Educational Supplement
John Marshall	Head teacher St Thomas More School
Anne Mason	Team Leader School Inclusion Department for Education and Skills
Margaret McEvoy	Economic Adviser Evaluation Team Social Analysis and Research Department for Education and Skills
Julie McGrane	Teacher and Ph.D. student St. Thomas More School
Andrew Morris	R&D Manager Learning and Skills Development Agency
Kathy Murphy	Social Analysis and Research Department for Education and Skills
Professor Ann Oakley	EPPI Centre University of London, Institute of Education
Dr. Tim Oates	Head of Research Qualifications and Curriculum Authority
Sir Michael Peckham	Chair of the National Educational Research Forum
Professor Sally Power	Head of the Institute of Education's School of Educational Foundations and Policy Studies
Professor Gareth Rees	University of Cardiff Building Research Capacity initiative, ESRC
Charles Ritchie	Social Analysis and Research Department for Education and Skills
Dr. Catrin Roberts	Assistant Director (Education) The Nuffield Foundation

Mary Russell	Universities Council for the Education of Teachers
Dr. Lesley Saunders	Policy Adviser Research General Teaching Council
Professor Tom Schuller	Centre for Wider Benefits of Learning (Institute of Education/Birkbeck College)
Judy Sebba	Senior Advisor on Research Department for Education and Skills
Professor Geoff Southworth	Head of Research National College for School Leadership
Meryl Thompson	Head of Policy Association of Teachers and Lecturers
John Traxler	Centre for ICT in Education Delta Institute University of Wolverhampton
Professor James Tooley	University of Newcastle Department of Education
Michele Weatherburn	Senior Research Officer Analytical Services Social Analysis and Research Department for Education and Skills
Cherry White	Senior Support Officer (Research Team) Teacher Training Agency
Professor Geoff Whitty	Director of the London Institute of Education
Ian Wilkinson	Teacher St. Thomas More School
Ianthe Wright	Team Leader/Teaching Assistant Department for Education and Skills
Martin Young	Head Teacher Cranford Park Primary School

ISBN 92-64-10030-X
New Challenges for Educational Research
© OECD 2003

PART I

Chapter 3

Education Research and Development in England

Background report by the Department for Education and Skills, England
May 2002

Abstract. *This chapter presents the background report prepared by the Department for Education and Skills, England for the OECD review of England's educational R&D system. It analyses national policies and agendas for educational R&D, how they are generated and the organisation and resources of the educational R&D system. It, furthermore, explores whether educational R&D is perceived to be relevant to policy-makers and practitioners, evidence of the impact on the improvement of policy and practice and how this is evaluated.*

3.1. Purpose of the review

The OECD has initiated reviews of research and development systems in different countries. In March 2001 the OECD undertook a review of educational research and development in New Zealand. In September 2001 they reported on this review that was subsequently discussed by the CERI Board. In May 2002 a similar review will be undertaken in England. This paper provides a general background for that review. Specific papers giving more detail in areas covered by this background paper have also been provided.

The purpose is to review the extent to which the educational research and development system within a country is functioning as an effective means for creating, collating and distributing the knowledge on which practitioners and policy-makers can draw. The aim is broader than a traditional educational research and development review focused on the quality of the research delivered. The focus will be on an evaluation of the contribution of educational research and development to the knowledge base of education in the emerging learning society. For the purposes of the review, educational research and development will be regarded as a multidisciplinary research field.

More specifically, the review will analyse national policies and agendas for educational research and development, how they are generated and the organisation and resources of the educational research and development system. It will explore whether educational research and development is perceived to be relevant to policy-makers and practitioners, evidence of the impact on the improvement of policy and practice and how this is evaluated. The interaction between researchers, teachers and policy-makers will be of particular interest as will the interaction with the international research community.

3.2. The context: education and the learning society in England

In a recent speech, Michael Barber (2001) head of the Prime Minister's delivery unit reiterated the determination of the government to pursue education reform and bring about a step change in the performance of the education service. Following the June 2001 election, Prime Minister Tony Blair reaffirmed his commitment to the delivery of improved education within the context of a wider reform of the public services as a whole. Indeed, he has placed delivery of reform of the public services at the centre of the agenda for the new Parliament. The goal is to ensure that all public services achieve consistently high standards and become increasingly tailored to the needs and aspirations of consumers. Only by doing so will they match the levels of quality that consumers have come to expect from the best businesses, while at the same time maintaining and strengthening an ethos of service to the public.

Michael Barber has argued that in order to deliver this level of performance, public services should:

- consistently achieve high minimum standards of performance and be held accountable for doing so;
- devolve resources and responsibility as far as possible to frontline units and staff in order to unleash their creativity and allow them to respond to the needs and aspirations of particular localities and communities;
- shape the pay, conditions and performance management of staff to enable the previous two objectives to be achieved;
- reward those who deliver and enable action to be taken in relation to those who do not;
- offer choice of both provider and types of provision as far as possible.

In education this has meant, for example, national and school targets, external inspection and self-review of schools and local education authorities, delegation and self management of schools and colleges, introduction of performance related pay for teachers, extending parental choice of schools and choice of service providers for schools.

The sense of urgency in education is reinforced not just by the belief that every passing day when a child's education is less than optimal is another day lost, but also the belief that time is running out for public education to prove its worth. The danger is that, as the economies of developed countries grow, more and more people will see private education for their children as a rational lifestyle option. If this were to occur, they would become correspondingly less willing to pay taxes to fund public education which, over time, would demoralise and reduce the quality of the service. Public education must deliver in order to achieve social cohesion and prevent ever-growing inequality from one generation to another.

England has the opportunity in the next five to ten years to achieve high standards across an entire system of 24 000 schools and over 7 million school students. The foundations for progress have been laid in recent years. Expenditure on education is increasing and after four years of progress with some hard evidence of improved outcomes, a start has been made. The challenge ahead remains substantial. For example, a major challenge ahead is ensuring the recruitment and retention of enough teachers of quality, in spite of the fact that more teachers started teaching in schools last September over the past seventeen years. Educational research and development has a key role in enhancing the status of the teaching profession through developing teachers as an evidence-informed profession.

3.3. Funding of educational research: sources and recipients

In the National Educational Research Forum's sub-group report on funding an attempt was made to map out existing funding and identify the overall budget. It is difficult to identify expenditure which counts only as "educational research" as distinguished from research in other areas of the social sciences or humanities. No central register of current research was kept at that time (although this has since been addressed – see CERUK below) so it impossible to obtain a clear overview of what research has already been done or is in progress. The second difficulty was that the major spender appeared to be central government but different and overlapping areas of government responsibility within the four countries of the UK mean that it is very difficult to clearly attribute spending to any one particular country. For example, the Higher Education Funding Council for England (HEFCE) is the biggest single funder and covers only England, as does the DfES, whereas the Research Councils have a UK-wide remit.

By using a combination of income and expenditure sources and inspired guesswork, the sub-group reached an estimate of about GBP 70-75 million per annum expenditure on educational research in England. This may sound considerable but the sub-group noted that it represents less than one half of one per cent of the total national expenditure on education.

The major source of funding is central government, either directly through departmental budgets, or via the Research Councils or through the Higher Education Funding Council for England (HEFCE). These bodies account for about 80% of the total spend. The main individual sources of this funding as shown in the chart below (provided by Jim Hillage for the sub-group) are as follows:

- The annual allocation for research and scholarship from HEFCE that is distributed by means of the quality-related Research Assessment Exercise (RAE). This source is estimated to account for up to 60% of the total spend.

- Central and Local Government probably contribute about a further 14% of the total. Their expenditure is policy related and tends to be directed towards "applied" rather than "pure" research.

- Income from Research Councils – about 5% of the total. The biggest spender in this category is the ESRC which funds research studentship, standalone responsive mode grants and fellowships. It also supports research programmes, centres and groups addressing identified priority topics and manages the UK wide Teaching and Learning Programme which with a current budget of approx GBP 25 million is the largest single research programme in education in the UK. The Council estimates that just over half its expenditure on education research take the form of finance for specific programmes, one third goes on standalone grants and fellowships and the rest on dedicated Research Centres.

- Income from charities represents about 7% of the total. These charities reflect a range of priorities and fund research in Universities, schools and by voluntary agencies. Some fund on a local basis, some are England only and some support projects throughout the UK.

- The balance is made up of income from EU projects, industry and other sources including a wide range of private sector educational and training organisations.

Indications are that 90% of the work is undertaken within university departments of education; while there are at least 100 separate institutions conducting educational research, 80% of the funding from government, charities and Research Councils goes to 22 institutions. This is a consequence both of the RAE system, which focuses on excellence, and external funding decisions. Relevant research is also conducted within other university departments and outside the higher education sector by government in various forms and by independent research institutes (*e.g.* the National Foundation for Educational Research). Finally there is research conducted by teachers and others, often as part of research degrees or increasingly through small scholarships (see below).

A report (*Cross cutting study of science research funding: analysis, arguments and proposals*) reviewing science and research published by the Treasury in 2000 noted that publicly funded science is increasingly important for the UK's innovation and productivity performance in a globalising knowledge economy. It noted the evidence of links between science and economic growth. A key recommendation was that current spending on the UK science base should at least be kept constant and that there is a strong case for increasing the volume of research undertaken.

3.4. Reviews of educational research and development

In 1995, the Teacher Training Agency (TTA) began to develop a range of strategies to promote teaching as a research-informed profession. In 1996, they invited David Hargreaves to give their annual lecture (*Teaching as a research-based profession: possibilities and prospects*) in which he compared the quality of educational research unfavourably with that of medicine. He argued that educational research is non-cumulative, that there is an unhelpful distinction between researchers and users, promotion in education has been de-coupled from both practitioner expertise and knowledge of research and that educational research is poor value in terms of improving the quality of education in schools. This was not a new debate and indeed Hargreaves himself had described "...educational research as generally disappointing...." In an earlier publication (Hargreaves, 1994) but it fuelled an ongoing discussion within the research community. Over the next few years the quality and impact of educational research was considered in detail in many sources (e.g. Edwards, 2000; Furlong, 1998; Gray, 1998; Mortimore and Mortimore, 1999; Rudduck and MacIntyre, 1998).

In 1998 two reviews of educational research were published. The first commissioned by Ofsted (Tooley and Darby, 1998) was an analysis of the quality of research publications while the second (Hillage et al., 1998) was commissioned by the Department for Education and Employment to analyse the direction, organisation, funding, quality and impact of educational research. This latter report concluded that the relationship between research, policy and practice needed to be improved. One of its conclusions was to suggest that the research agenda was too supplier driven and that this was exacerbated by the process of research funding. The review noted that the overemphasis on short term evaluations at the expense of exploration and development in government-sponsored research meant that research was following, rather than leading policy.

While the OECD review focuses on the use of knowledge rather than on the quality of research, the Hillage et al. review made clear that the shortcomings in the quality of some research was limiting its use. They noted that the research that addressed issues relevant to policy and practice was too small scale, incapable of generating findings that are generalisable, insufficiently based on existing knowledge and inaccessible. Pressure on researchers to produce empirical findings in published journals of international repute reflected different priorities to those which "users" in the system need to inform policy and practice. Dissemination of findings was described as "rampant ad hocery" with little evidence of a strategy or concerted approach. The report concluded that a lack of interest and understanding of research among policy-makers and practitioners, the absence of a capacity to use findings and lack of a system for using evidence in policy-making limited the impact of research on policy and practice.

The review had a mixed reception. Funders, users and some researchers welcomed it. Other researchers were critical of the methodology describing it as "quick and dirty" or considered that it was too easy to blame the researchers predominantly for problems that the authors had acknowledged needed to be addressed by all stakeholders. Furthermore, some felt that the impact of research was greater than that described in the report but not recognised where it was implicit rather than explicit. An example of this is when teacher educators refer to teaching practices without making specific reference to the research that has informed them or teachers use research-based curriculum materials.

The Department for Education and Employment drew up an action plan to address each of the recommendations in the report. The current Department for Education and Skills (DfES) research strategy reflects further developments of this action plan. The review prompted and highlighted the need for a research strategy but the wider context should be acknowledged. Since 1997 government departments in England have embarked on a process of modernising government which has promoted the use of evidence in the policy process. The Centre for Management and Policy Studies in the Cabinet Office and the Civil Service College within it have developed a programme for senior civil servants and ministers designed to promote a better understanding of evidence and how it should be used.

The wider international context is important. Furlong and White (2002) have recently undertaken a review of current educational research capacity in Wales commissioned by Universities Council for the Education of Teachers (Cymru). The National Research Council in US published a study (Shavelson and Towne, 2001) to examine and clarify the nature of scientific inquiry in education and how the federal government can best foster and support it. The Scottish Educational Research Association (Kirkwood, 2002) is considering how best to encourage further developments of a research strategy for Scotland. Many of the issues identified in the Hillage *et al.* review and reflected in the DfES's research strategy, are noted in all these reports and are in no sense unique to England.

3.5. The DfES research strategy

The review of educational research identified two underlying themes which needed to be addressed; better use of the current evidence base and greater investment in a high quality evidence base for the future. Each of the components in the research strategy contributes to one or both of these overarching aims. The DfES research budget has nearly doubled since 1997 and one third of it is now invested in the strategic initiatives described in this paper with the remaining two thirds spent on individual research projects. The DfES evaluations of policy are funded through programme budgets controlled by policy teams but are quality assured and monitored by the research teams. Much of the work on Information and Communication Technology (ICT) is funded through this stream.

Dedicated research centres

The Hillage *et al.* review identified the need for research centres of excellence. Consultation suggested that concentrating more resources in a few centres based in single institutions would contribute little to the development of research capacity or interdisciplinarity. Hence it was decided to invest in "dedicated" research centres dedicated in their focus on a particular area but cross-institutional and interdisciplinary drawing on the key researchers in a given field wherever they are based. These centres involve collaborative teams of researchers from different disciplines and institutions working on a longer term research programme for 3-5 years. This will enable sustained work in priority areas to establish better quality evidence and continuity. A sustained programme of research also enables theoretical advances to develop alongside shorter term practical and evaluative research. Research capacity can be built through the different disciplines working together and thereby extending their skills and through studentships and attachments. The centres provide a focal point for information and discussion for other researchers, ministers, civil servants and practitioners, encouraging debate, challenge and greater mutual understanding of the issues. The investment involved in these centres is considerable – an average of GBP 1 million per centre for the first three years, renewable for a further two years.

Two dedicated research centres began work in 2000. The first is focused on the *wider benefits of learning* and is directed by Professor John Bynner and Professor Andy Green at the Institute of Education and Professor Tom Schuller at Birkbeck College, University of London. It is researching the non-economic benefits that learning brings to the individual learner and to society as a whole. The overall programme covers health, ageing, family and parenting, crime, citizenship and participation and leisure and lifestyle. It is undertaking methodological work on models and measures that have been used to assess the social benefits of learning alongside data analysis on indicators of social cohesion and quality of life. For example, one recent research report (Bynner *et al.*, 2001) noted that when controlled for earlier family circumstances and educational achievement, individuals who are engaged in adult learning suffer less from poor health and are more likely to be active citizens.

The second centre focuses on the *economics of education* and is directed by Professor Steve Machin at the London School of Economics. It also involves the Institute for Fiscal Studies and Institute of Education bringing together researchers from economics, education and other social sciences. A major strand of this centre's work has been on the methodological challenge of developing cost effectiveness measures of educational interventions. The areas of research include the production and supply of education and skills, the demand for education and skills and the returns to education and skills. One project looked at participation in post-compulsory education and found that it is unlikely to increase further without marked improvement in examination results or major increases in youth unemployment as a result of an economic recession. Further analysis revealed that while prior attainment strongly determined the level of qualification attained, the type of qualification was more likely to be influenced by family characteristics and regional conditions. Another project is looking at the effects of lifelong learning on future income and employment experiences.

A third centre that began its work in 2001 focuses on *Information and Communication Technology (ICT)*. It is directed by Professor Steve Molyneux at the University of Wolverhampton in association with the Learning Lab, a not-for-profit centre (funded by a number of IT and telecom companies). This centre will look at the impact of levels and type of access to ICT on social and educational inclusion, initially for adult learners.

A fourth centre, the National Research and Development Centre for Adult Literacy and Numeracy, has been established as part of the Adult Basic Skills Strategy to develop the knowledge base on how to improve literacy and numeracy and the impact of this on individuals and the economy. It involves a consortium led by the Institute of Education, University of London together with other universities including Sheffield. It is funded by the DfES's Adult Basic Skills Strategy Unit

The Learning and Skills Development Agency who are independent of government have established a National Research Centre for Learning and Skills. This was a response to concerns that further education, adult and community learning are under-researched. The new Learning and Skills Research Centre will help address the gaps in our knowledge and strengthen the evidence base.

Longitudinal Studies

The Department's research programme is currently supporting 10 longitudinal studies. Two major developments for example are:

- A project group is taking forward plans to launch a major new longitudinal survey of 14-21 year olds which will bring together in one study previously separate proposals for surveys of young people, young ethnic minorities and of potential entrants to higher education. The project is seen as a potential successor to the current Youth Cohort Survey.

- The Millennium Cohort, led by the Economic and Social Research Council (ESRC), is a new longitudinal study to which the DfES is contributing. The main fieldwork commenced last autumn, surveying 20 000 babies born between July 2000 and June 2001. DfES is contributing GBP 200k per annum to the survey. Other government departments and the Office for National Statistics are also co-funding. The study will provide a vital comparison sample for the evaluation of Sure Start (major new programme for early intervention).

These longer term studies provide an opportunity for more proactive research questions to be addressed and for complex issues that may be misinterpreted through shorter term perspectives to be researched. Again, the sustained focus on a given area should enable researchers to develop their theoretical understanding of these issues alongside generating research findings for shorter term application. The Department is continuing to provide collaborative funding for the major birth cohort and household studies.

International Studies

The DfES participates in a number of collaborative international studies which provide insights into the factors affecting achievement and opportunity. These include:

- OECD programme for developing indicators on student achievement (PISA).
- Progress in International Reading Literacy (PIRLS).
- Third International Study of Science and Maths (TIMSS) repeat.
- IEA citizenship study.

Richard Bartholomew, the chief research officer of the DfES represents the UK on the CERI board of OECD and we are participating in a number of OECD initiatives including that on brain research and learning, knowledge management, schooling for tomorrow and the proposed work on teacher recruitment, retention and development.

International researchers are involved in DfES externally commissioned work. For example, a team of researchers from Ontario and Manitoba led by Professor Michael Fullan has been commissioned to undertake a four year evaluation of the national literacy and numeracy strategies in primary education. Professor Peter Cuttance from Australia is involved in the evaluation of the key stage 3 national strategy. Many of the research review groups registered with the EPPI centre have corresponding members in other countries and of course the literature reviewed is drawn from international sources with a couple of the review groups managing to include some studies reported in languages other than English.

The DfES is represented at international research conferences. Representatives attend the annual British Educational Research Association conference, which attracts considerable attendance from abroad. Symposia on the research strategy and on the systematic review work have been featured at these conferences for the last three years. Judy Sebba, Senior Adviser (Research) participated in a ROLE program panel at the National Science Foundation (NSF) assessing research proposals as part of the reciprocal arrangement between the Economic and Social Research Council, Teaching and Learning Programme (see below) and the NSF. We have agreed to submit a proposal for a joint symposium with the NSF to next year's American Educational Research Association conference.

3.6. The National Educational Research Forum: developing a framework for research

The remit of the National Educational Research Forum is to provide strategic direction for educational research in England and to raise the quality, profile and impact of educational research. Its key objective is to develop a national framework within which a more coherent, better quality and relevant research programme in education can develop.

The Forum was set up by the DfES in September 1999. The independent chair was appointed by the Secretary of State and members were appointed by an independent panel led by the chair following open advertisement. It currently has 19 members including two teachers and one teacher organisation representative and is chaired by Sir Michael Peckham, previously Director of the School of Public Policy at University College London and a key figure in the development of the NHS research and development strategy. Five sub-groups focussing on priorities, funding, capacity, quality and impact consulted literature, unpublished reports and expert witnesses to inform its first consultation document.

The Forum published a consultation document in November 2000 outlining possible components of a strategy. It invited individuals, institutions and organisations from within the UK and overseas to contribute actively and imaginatively with suggestions, analyses and ideas. Over 100 responses to the consultation were received and analysed. Two national consultation conferences were held and meetings held with specific groups who were under-represented in the responses such as parents and employers. In September 2001, the Forum redrafted and published its strategy document in the light of the consultation responses. These proposals were warmly received. The proposals include establishing a priorities group, dedicated education foresight, a funders' forum, improving research capacity, reviewing of training and improving the knowledge base and access to it, all of which are discussed in the rest of this paper.

3.7. Funders' Forum

The National Educational Research Forum's strategy document proposed the setting up of a Funders' Forum to coordinate the efforts of individual funders, establish greater sustainability of funding and explore possibilities for greater collaboration between funders. It also suggested exploring ways in which major research funders who have not funded research in education might be persuaded to do so and how university departments other than education can be funded to undertake educational research. The Funders' Forum set up by the National Educational Research Forum met for the first time in November 2001 and has recently had a further meeting. Sir Brian Fender, previously chief executive of the Higher Education Funding Council for

England chairs the Funders' Forum. Organisations that fund educational research were all invited to join the forum and 29 organisations did so.

At the first two meetings they compared the research interests of individual member organisations and discussed their role in dissemination and impact including knowledge management. They have undertaken a funders' mapping exercise to share information about the rationale, mission, current programme of research activities, types of studies funded, strategies for enhancing participation by users and strategies for measuring impact.

3.8. Establishing priorities in education

The Forum proposes to establish an education priorities group to develop a methodology and criteria for setting priorities for research and development in education. This group will advise the National Educational Research Forum on priority issues in education. This advice will form part of the information made available to research funders, researchers and other interests. The chair of the Forum has invited Professor Charles Desforges, a member of the Forum to chair the priorities group and membership will reflect the range of constituencies in education. Both the Forum and the priorities group will also be informed by analytic workshops that are being set up to look at key issues in education such as the impact of buildings on learning and innovation in education.

The Forum will establish an Education Observatory to examine current and emergent developments as well as medium and longer-term trends likely to shape the future. The Observatory will assume responsibility for taking forward the Foresight proposals outlined in the strategy document. The outputs of the Observatory will inform the activities of the Education Priorities Group and the Forum.

Education needs a dedicated Observatory/Foresight exercise to enable it to be prepared to shape future changes. Its focus will be the learning society, placing learning at its centre wherever it takes place, be that an institution, the home or a workplace. It will look at the national and international context, and at formal and informal learning. It will consider differences in class, gender and race and ensure that differentiation is made between different social groups. It also needs to be focussed on the role that research can play in helping us be prepared for the future, and in informing us as to what we need to know. The Forum has synthesised the outcomes of other Foresight exercises so as to complement rather than duplicate them. The Forum is in the process of identifying a possible chair and members for this exercise with the intention that the group will produce a report within 18 months of starting their work.

3.9. Investing in the future evidence base

Developing systematic reviews in education

In response to the recommendation in the Hillage *et al.* review and informed by the experiences of the international Cochrane Collaboration in healthcare intervention, the DfES has made a significant investment in systematic reviewing. The Evidence for Policy and Practice Information and Co-ordinating Centre (EPPI), directed by Professor Ann Oakley at the Social Science Research Unit was set up for five years to provide centralised resources and support for those wishing to undertake systematic reviews around what is known about a range of educational policy and practice issues.

Systematic reviewing involves identifying research reports through electronic searching and other means and assessing them in an explicit and transparent way so as to produce accessible, relevant and quality-assured syntheses of research findings. Research employing the full range of methods is included in the reviews. The EPPI centre has been running for just over two years. It has developed guidelines for carrying out systematic reviews, criteria for data extraction and inclusion and exclusion of studies and training and support for the review groups as well as influencing the wider research community through disseminating methodological developments. Groups have been self selected to date but include researchers, policy-makers and practitioners. The groups have been strongly encouraged to include the widest possible range of research perspectives in particular, researchers known to disagree in order to increase the credibility of the reviews. One recent group to register, looking at continuing professional development for teachers was instigated, and is led by, a major teacher organisation.

There are ten review groups now registered including assessment, leadership and management, inclusion, gender, English teaching, further education, early years, thinking skills, modern foreign languages and continuing professional development. Each of the six groups who registered in the first year undertook one review. The review questions were:

- The impact of summative assessment and tests on pupils' motivation for learning?

- The impact of ICT on literacy learning in English 5-16?

- A systematic review of the effectiveness of school-level actions for promoting participation by all students?

- The impact of financial circumstances on engagement with post-16 learning?

- The impact of leadership and management on school achievement?

- What kind of strategies improve equal opportunities relating to gender for pupils in mixed sex primary schools?

Summaries of the reviews for policy-makers, teachers, lecturers, researchers, parents, governors and students as appropriate to the topic are being prepared by representatives from those groups.

Insofar as this work has been publicised to date, it is recognised to be ground-breaking. These will be the first systematic reviews in education to incorporate a full range of methodologies. The keywording system developed by the EPPI centre was adopted in the review of research capacity in Wales and the review manual and techniques are attracting international interest. In England, the resistance from some researchers that was apparent when the centre was commissioned has reduced although is still evident. There are concerns that by focusing on "what works" that the reviews will be atheoretical. There are still concerns that too much weight will be given to quantitative studies and that a single view of "best practice" will be promoted. This latter fear could only be realised if the reviews were to conclude that the research indicated one unequivocal answer on each review question which seems unlikely to occur. There is a view that funders will limit the scope of future research according to the EPPI criteria or the gaps identified by the reviews but the diversity of funders and their determination to remain independent of government suggests they will continue to fund a broad range of issues.

Some clear challenges have emerged from the experiences of these groups in completing their first reviews. The process is rigorous but cumbersome demanding major time commitment and substantial coordination between those involved. The groups have received a small grant of GBP 20 000 towards each of these first reviews with funding reducing to GBP 15 000 for subsequent reviews, in recognition that the first reviews received less support as the system was being developed. The groups have indicated that the true costs are nearer GBP 70-80 000. A key challenge for the longer term is to establish multiple funding streams to support reviews as occurs in the international Cochrane Collaboration and to ensure that systematic reviews are recognised as high status scholarly activity in the assessment and funding of research.

The work on systematic reviews is providing the basis of important debate on methods and purpose. The methodological developments have begun to influence funders in their commissioning and reviewing of research proposals. For example, the criteria in the EPPI manual offer a basis for reviewing proposed methodology. The review groups provide a real opportunity to bring together not only competing research interests but the differing perspectives of researchers, policy-makers and practitioners. In a couple of months we will begin to see whether the reviews succeed in their most important but hardest test – that of being accessible and influencing policy and practice.

Developing systematic reviews in the social sciences: the ESRC evidence-based network

Professor Ken Young and colleagues are undertaking further work on approaches to systematic reviewing at Queen Mary and Westfield College, University of London funded by the Economic and Social Research Council. The Centre began in December 2000, and is both undertaking research itself and supporting a network of seven research teams across Britain not focused specifically on education. This evidence network is committed to developing the knowledge base and building access pathways to it for the user community. This will be done primarily through the mechanism of systematic reviews but also via less complex, time consuming and costly narrative reviews, methodological and conceptual papers, bibliographic listings and critiques in order to satisfy the differing needs and timescales of the initiative's potential clients. The ESRC funding enables a number of researcher-driven activities to be undertaken and currently these include:

- At Queen Mary, a bibliography on evidence-based practice, a map of relevant organisations and individuals to whom the Network will relate, a review of training provision for both researchers and practitioners and factors affecting the implementation of guidelines for professional practice.

- Across centres within the network, a range of studies, including a discussion paper on EBP requirements (St Andrews), research relevant to children (Barnardos/City/York), the work recruitment and retention of ill and disabled people (Glasgow), and the effects of residential turnover (Glasgow/Bristol).

Regular contact between the team at Queen Mary and Westfield and the EPPI centre takes place to ensure complementary progress.

Current Educational Research in the UK (CERUK) database

Hillage *et al.* noted that educational research and development was insufficiently based on existing knowledge. Policy-makers, practitioners and researchers complained of the lack of access to comprehensive databases of current and published research. Current Educational Research in the UK (CERUK) is a freely available database developed by a partnership between the National Foundation for Educational Research (NFER) and the EPPI centre, co-funded by the DfES. It links closely with the comprehensive databases of educational research and reviews that are being developed by the EPPI centre.

It holds information on educational research projects which are being undertaken in the UK covering pre-school, school, FE, HE, adult, lifelong and continuing education. It was launched at the BERA conference in September 2001 and has been warmly welcomed. The DfES makes it a requirement of their research contracts that details are logged on to the database and other funders are considering doing the same. It is an attempt to ensure that funders, researchers and users can access what is going on and that related projects can assist one another rather than wasting resources through unintended overlap.

The Economic and Social Research Council (ESRC) Teaching and Learning Programme

The ESRC are managing a GBP 25 million programme of research on teaching and learning funded by top-sliced HEFCE money and contributions from the Welsh Office, the Scottish Office and DfES. The first phase of the programme funded research networks across institutions focusing on inclusion, science education, pupil perspectives and work related learning. Following extensive consultation with users and researchers, phase 2 focused on motivation and engagement in learning processes, transforming research on cognition to promote learning and developing learning communities. A further nine projects were funded in this phase including work on further education, enhancing teaching and learning in undergraduate courses and learning in the workplace. Phase 3 is focusing on post-compulsory education and outline bids are being reviewed.

The ESRC programme criteria stipulate involvement of users in every part of the research process: identifying research priorities, commissioning projects, conducting the research and evaluating outcomes. The requirements also emphasise the need to identify clear outcomes for learners and contributions that the research will make to building research capacity which is supported by a further major strand of the programme described later in this paper. Applications are expected to build in plans for dissemination and impact.

3.10. Evaluating and improving the quality of educational research and development

The Research Assessment Exercise (RAE)

The Research Assessment Exercise (RAE) is the main mechanism by which research quality is assessed and funding allocated. Researchers submit a selection of their "best" publications (in terms of international, academic excellence) to the education subject panel representing the Higher Education Funding Council (HEFCE). In the Hillage et al. review concerns were raised that researchers find this process conflicts with the demands to disseminate research in ways that might impact on policy and practice. In 1998, the HEFCE set up a task force to explore membership of the research assessment exercise education panel and the application of the criteria for the RAE in 2001. The report recommended to the Chair of the panel that a quarter of the members should be users of research, in particular teachers. This recommendation was implemented although only one of the four users was a teacher. The users prepared a report on their experiences.

A second recommendation was that greater emphasis be placed on the impact of research on policy and practice. The criteria were revised to recognise curriculum, teaching and assessment material where justified by the underlying research. The criteria also suggested that the quality of research will often be demonstrated through its influence on other researchers, policy-makers and practitioners. These changes are significant in providing the basis for high quality, relevant and practical research to be credited. Further work will need to be done to ensure that high quality research reviews are adequately recognised in this process. In particular, where different disciplines are involved, collaborators from disciplines other than education submit their work to other subject panels whose criteria reflect less recognition of applied research. The outcomes of the 2001 RAE were announced in December and more recently, the translation of the ratings into funding allocations have been met with strong concerns in the universities due to the limits imposed. There are concerns that too much concentration of resource fails to allow for nurturing of emerging areas of excellence.

Journal Editors' Conference

Peer review is the main mechanism for assessing the quality of research and given the focus of the RAE on published papers in academic journals, of subsequent funding allocations. The quality and consistency of peer review has been debated for many years internationally and in every discipline. It was raised as an issue in the Hillage *et al.* review in connection with the RAE and more generally. In November 2000, under the auspices of the National Educational Research Forum and initiated by five journal editors, a conference was held for journal editors in education and included colleagues from Scotland and Wales. Inputs were provided on the work of the Forum in particular, about different ways of considering dissemination of research and on the systematic review work. Lively debate took place on the role of editors, the quality of manuscripts submitted, issues relating to peer review and the impact of the RAE on publishing. A second journal editors' conference is being held in May and inputs on the 2001 RAE and on peer review are being made.

Advisory panels

The DfES set up research advisory panels following other attempts to widen the participation on research priorities (such as open advertisements in the press which produced some 300 responses). There are three panels addressing early years and schooling, education and skills for 14-19 year olds and higher education, workforce development and skills. On each panel there are 7-10 leading researchers and about the same number of research analysts from the DfES. The DfES chief economist, Paul Johnson, chairs all three panels.

The purpose of the panels is to advise the department about priority areas for research and discuss the latest research evidence drawing out the implications for future work. Two meetings of each panel have been held to date and from feedback received it is proposed to extend their role to include identifying priorities and shaping the research programme, helping to develop research specifications through literature reviews and advisory work on methodology, and peer reviewing tenders and reports and undertaking and discussing reviews of evidence in key current topic areas.

The National Teacher Research Panel

The Teacher Research Panel was established by a partnership between the DfES and TTA. It is a group of teachers who have research experience and expertise and are consulted in determining research priorities, commissioning research, contributing to steering groups and assisting in more effective dissemination strategies. In the ESRC funded Teaching and Learning Programme they contributed to reviewing the large number of proposals submitted in phase 2 and there was clear evidence of their influence. In March 2001, they made a major contribution to a very successful national conference about evidence-informed policy and practice attended by more than 300 teachers and in December 2001 contributed to the first annual DfES research conference. They have prepared papers about teachers' perspectives on research for international conferences. The current chair of the panel Jill Wilson, is also a member of the National Educational Research Forum.

3.11. Capacity building

The National Educational Research Forum proposed a review of existing training programmes in research skills for researchers and teachers. This is being undertaken through the documentation that is available from accreditation recognition procedures. The ESRC teaching and learning programme has a major strand of work on building capacity and the Forum is collaborating with them on reviewing research skills amongst researchers. The Forum recently produced a discussion paper on capacity building (Dyson and Desforges, 2002) to stimulate further debate and proposals.

The ESRC Teaching and Learning Programme Research Capacity Building Network

This network was set up to build capacity in particular, in research skills in the research community. Professor Stephen Gorard and colleagues at the Cardiff University School of Social Sciences lead it and have produced helpful papers and newsletters. The key aims of the network are to promote and extend multidisciplinary and multi-sector research in teaching and learning, to enhance system-wide capacity for research based practice and to develop the capability to transform the knowledge base relevant into practice. Initially, it is working with the researchers involved in the 14 projects in the ESRC Teaching and Learning Programme and those preparing bids for phase 3 of the programme which focuses on post-compulsory education.

The activities include setting up training events, workshops, discussions and publications. Its main focus is needs-directed training provision although it is acknowledged that there is a shortage of particular skills within the range of methodologies required. For example, there are increasing opportunities to interrogate large datasets but too few researchers with the range of skills and experience to do so effectively. Similarly, complex issues being researched in education often require combining quantitative and qualitative skills yet there are insufficient researchers trained and experienced in both. Techniques such as multilevel modelling and software for analysing qualitative data had not yet developed when most of the research community in education undertook their initial research training. This initiative is contributing to the capacity of educational research and development to tackle more complex research questions and increase potential impact on policy and practice in the future.

Coordinating capacity across government

The Hillage *et al.* review suggested that research activity across government within education lacked coordination. In 1998 we set up a research liaison group to coordinate effort across the government agencies working on educational research. Twice termly meetings are held of the DfES, Ofsted, QCA and TTA to ensure better coordination of our research programmes and greater consistency in commissioning and quality control procedures. Once a year this meeting is attended by a wider group of organisations including the GTC, National College of School Leadership and others who are independent of government. Twice a year the chief executives of these organisations meet to discuss their research and development strategies.

3.12. Capacity for practitioners to engage in research

TTA school-based research consortia

The TTA school-based research consortia initiative included two secondary and two primary partnerships funded by the TTA and the Centre for British Teachers to support teacher engagement in and with research as a means of improving teaching and enhancing learning. The consortia, involving classroom teachers, their schools, HEIs and LEAs, each took a specific theme:

- Manchester and Salford Schools Consortium – a primary consortium focusing on literacy, numeracy and science.
- Leeds Primary Schools Consortium – a primary consortium focusing on numeracy and literacy;

- Norwich Area Schools Consortium – a secondary consortium focusing on overcoming disaffection;

- North East School Based Research Consortium – a secondary consortium focusing on critical thinking skills.

The partnerships have developed a range of evidence, activities and resources relating both to their specific themes and to the development of research related partnerships. The success of this scheme has been in the partnerships it has established both within each network between schools, local education authorities and higher education and beyond the network to other institutions.

A strategy for the continuing professional development of teachers

In 2001, following a consultation on professional development, the DfES published *Learning and Teaching: A strategy for Professional Development*. This was warmly welcomed by teachers and researchers who noted that in addition to creating more opportunities for teachers to engage in research, the professional development it was advocating was itself informed by research. For example, the strategy notes that teachers learning from and with each other and from evidence are the most effective ways to build professional skills. It outlined the range of professional development opportunities for teachers and the support available for them. Three of the initiatives – Best Practice Research Scholarships, professional bursaries and sabbaticals are all potential routes to support to use or undertake research although the scholarships is the route designed to do so explicitly.

Teacher Research Grant Scheme and best practice research scholarships

The TTA Teacher Research Grant Scheme aimed to contribute to the development of a cumulative stock of high-quality, small-scale, classroom-based research carried out by teachers, to raise other teachers' interest in research and evidence, and to extend the debate about the role of teachers in classroom research in order to raise standards and improve classroom practice. Teachers awarded grants undertook classroom-based research over a period of one academic year. Each project was undertaken with the support of a mentor from higher education or a local education authority to help with research methods, access to existing research and evidence and to ensure clarity of focus and direction. On completion of their project, teachers submitted both a report and a summary aimed at providing easily accessible information for colleagues to whet teachers' appetite for finding out more.

Following a pilot involving 27 grants in 1996-97, over a hundred grants of GBP 2 500 for a teacher working alone or GBP 3 500 for collaborative projects were funded during 1998-2001. Summaries of findings of their work are available from the TTA and examples are on the website. After the pilot phase, the TTA gave particular emphasis to projects which build cumulatively on previously established research and evidence by testing or exploring specific, identified evidence from previous enquiries. From 2000, the TTA's remit became focused on recruitment, initial training and induction so the continuing professional development work transferred elsewhere. The DfES began the Best Practice Research Scholarships in 1999 building on the experience of the Teacher Research Grant Scheme.

The Best Practice Research Scholarships programme (BPRS) is one of a series of initiatives supporting teachers' continuing professional development. To contribute to teachers' continuing professional development and to encourage the sharing of best practice, teachers in England are offered up to GBP 2 500 to undertake sharply focused inquiries into classroom practice. The criteria require teachers applying to specify how the work will impact on learning outcomes and to describe plans for dissemination and impact. There are over 2000 teachers in receipt of the scholarships and many of the reports submitted have been disseminated at conferences, training sessions and in professional journals although a significant proportion of teachers who have completed their scholarships have not yet produced their reports.

National Union of Teachers' Scholarships

The Teacher2Teacher programme provides opportunities for teachers to meet other teachers and learn more about various aspects of teaching and learning. Teachers then have the chance to try out and evaluate particular teaching strategies in their own classrooms. The programmes support teachers in carrying out research and investigations, passing on their findings to other teachers, and contributing to professional knowledge about teaching and learning.

Twelve pairs of teachers working with all ages of children in the North of England have been awarded NUT-funded scholarships to investigate the effective teaching of thinking skills. The Union has established a partnership with the Education Department at Newcastle University which has expertise in teaching thinking skills and supporting school-based projects. Over approximately 20 weeks, teachers have been trialling and evaluating the teaching of thinking skills in their classrooms. Support from tutors is provided by telephone/e-mail. A network has been set up for teachers involved in thinking skills projects.

NCSL Networked Learning Communities

The National College of School Leadership is promoting practitioner research through a range of means including attached research associates and support for the development of networked learning communities. Networked Learning Communities are purposeful social entities that are characterised by a commitment to quality, rigour, and a focus on outcomes. They are also an effective means of supporting innovation in times of change. In education, Networked Learning Communities promote the dissemination of good practice, enhance the professional development of teachers including use of and involvement in research, support capacity building in schools and mediate between centralised and decentralised structures.

British Educational Research Association (BERA)/ESRC fellowships

Capacity building in educational research is partly limited by the current profile of educational researchers. Two thirds of the current academic educational research community are over 50 years old and insufficient young graduates are being attracted into research as a career. In 1999, BERA put a proposal to ministers for the possibility of support for research fellowships. The scheme developed is intended for established, practising teachers, local education authority staff or others working in the education service who want to do a part-time Phd but may continue to work in education, change to a research career or combine research and practice in the future. The scheme is administered through the ESRC Teaching and Learning Initiative and those registered are attached to one of the projects or networks in the programme to ensure adequate training and support. Funding is provided to support a combination of full or part-time release for the full-time equivalent of not more than 28 months over a period of up to five years. Two individuals started on the scheme in October 2001 and a further two will begin later this year. Other schemes for attracting graduates into research include Phd attachments to the dedicated research centres.

Students as researchers

There has been a growing interest in the role of school students themselves in research. The ultimate test of the accessibility of research might be, for example, students using the outcomes of systematic reviews to discuss or even challenge the teaching approaches used in their lessons. But involving students as researchers has been demonstrated to be a powerful catalyst to school improvement (Raymond, 2001). Work at Sharnbrook Upper School in Bedfordshire suggests that data collected by students from other students may be more valid and reliable. In a school in which the ethos of "pupil voice" is well developed it can also lead to significant changes in the school curriculum. The theme of student voice is the focus of a major research network within the ESRC Teaching and Learning Programme and is explored more fully in Fielding (2002).

3.13. Disseminating research to practitioners and other users

Research of the month

The General Teaching Council (GTC) is committed to developing teaching as a more evidence informed profession. It believes that teachers should be able to benefit more directly from others' research as well as supported in initiating their own. This is more likely to happen if teachers can engage with research rather than just read about it: we are trying to adopt a "pedagogical" model of research dissemination. So, the aim of *Research of the month* is to interrogate research on behalf of practitioners. Research is selected that, in the view of the GTC:

- illuminates the complex tasks involved in teaching;
- enables teachers to see clearly whether there are links with their own pupils and practice, and what these are;
- provides detailed information about the particular teaching and learning processes in classrooms with which teachers can identify;
- is written and presented as accessibly as possible, in case teachers want to obtain and read the original text.

For each topic, a team from the Centre for Using Research and Evidence in Education (CUREE) has reviewed, selected and summarised one or more published research studies. Each topic is presented and structured according to a series of questions that the GTC has designed to bring out the messages for teachers and teaching. Findings are illustrated by high quality case studies. The review criteria for selecting studies cover the readability and relevance of research as well as its ethical integrity and methodological quality.

Research summaries on the web

The Centre for the Use of Research and Evidence in Education (CUREE) is contracted to summarise research findings on the Standards Site of the DfES web site. They identify research and quality-assure it with particular consumers in mind for example, local education authority staff, teachers, lecturers and parents. Part of the work will be seeking to ensure that these groups are able to feed in their priority areas of research. Researchers will be invited to summarise their research in 3-4 pages giving further sources. Around 25 such summaries will be lodged on the site each year. Comments will be invited via the site and once the site is launched in the Autumn there may be areas that generate sufficient interest to set up discussion fora.

Research briefs and reports

The DfES is committed to publishing all research that it commissions. The full reports are available both on the website and in hard copy. All reports are summarised into four page research briefs again available on the web or in hard copy. A contact name with e-mail address is given on these research briefs and readers are invited to request further details. Experience suggests that some studies have generated much interest leading to requests for information for further research on that topic, speakers to attend conferences or training events and many practitioners pursuing part time higher degrees or full time students wanting further clarification or support.

Teachers' magazine

Teachers' magazine was launched in spring 1999 and is the DfES's magazine for the teaching profession in England. The magazine tackles the issues of the day for the teaching profession. It aims to be contemporary, challenging, thought-provoking, dynamic, interesting, informative, professional and entertaining. It aims to provide classroom teachers with an informative view of what is happening in school education. The magazine is aimed at all teachers in England. It is written for classroom teachers in the primary and secondary sectors, but heads of department, senior teachers and head teachers also form part of the readership. Since January 2002 there have been two versions of the magazine, one for primary and one for secondary teachers. It has a circulation of 360 000 – 230 000 copies are sent direct to teachers' homes and the rest are sent to schools. It carries articles about research sporadically but plans to increase the coverage of research are being considered.

Seminars and conferences

There has been a substantial increase in the activities focusing on practitioner research over the last few years. The annual BERA conference has more teachers contributing both about the process of teachers undertaking and using research and on specific research projects. Findings from the Teacher Training Agency funded school-based research consortia were recently reported at a national conference and a major conference on teachers and research was held in March 2001 also hosted by the Teacher Training Agency. The DfES held its first annual research conference in November 2001 at which teachers contributed sessions. Smaller seminars are held for senior policy-makers and ministers at which researchers summarise ongoing or recently completed research followed by questions and discussion.

3.14. The impact of research on policy and practice

The sub-group of the Forum that addressed impact distinguished clearly between dissemination and impact. Most existing activity could better be described as dissemination than impact and assumed rather than planned. There are a number of research studies that have had a clear impact on policy and in the longer term may be expected to influence practice. However, there are areas that are not served well by good quality research evidence, where research is inconclusive or in which the research evidence is not easily accessible. These factors may contribute to policies for which underlying research cannot easily be linked. There are other studies such as the work on pupil mobility (Dobson and Henthorne, 1999) which provide rich data but where the issues are highly complex and policy implications are conflicting making it more difficult to ensure appropriate action is taken. There is much progress to be made in developing the willingness and capacity of policy-makers to use evidence. However, some examples where impact has been apparent are provided here for illustrative purposes.

The impact of research on primary to secondary school transfer and teaching and learning for 11-14 year olds

The review of research and practice on transition and transfer (Galton, Gray and Rudduck, 1999) noted the poor progress made by pupils in years 7 and 8 and the drop in motivation that appears to contribute to this. The research evidence has informed policy and practice at national, local education authority and school levels. Nationally, the DfES introduced common transfer forms to ensure all schools receive minimum basic information to enable them to build on pupils' previous standards. The Qualifications and Curriculum Authority developed "bridging units" which are pieces of work that pupils begin in year 6 in the primary school and complete in their new school in year 7. Many local education authorities included transfer and transition in their Education Development Plans and many schools have further developed their strategies in this area. The second stage of this research is an intervention programme in which local education authorities and schools that have volunteered to do so, are introducing specific strategies and outcomes are being carefully monitored.

The main impact of the transition and transfer study was that it informed the National Key Stage 3 Strategy for 11-14 year olds. Together with international evidence on the middle years of schooling, it informed the teacher development programme. Evidence from studies and reviews of the effectiveness of approaches incorporating thinking skills (McGuinness,1999) and assessment for learning (Black and Wiliam, 1998, Wiliam and Lee, 2001, often referred to as formative assessment) which demonstrated increased motivation, pupil engagement and management of their own learning, further informed this strategy. In Autumn 2000, the strategy was introduced as a pilot, targeted at those teaching 11-14 year olds and included subject training, literacy and numeracy across the curriculum, assessment for learning and thinking skills. The strategy is being independently evaluated by a consortium of researchers from the universities of Bath, London and Melbourne.

Further support for this work was provided through revisions to the national curriculum in 2000 including thinking skills in the general requirements, published schemes of work and development of resources. Thinking skills and assessment for learning were also prioritised in the guidelines for applicants for Best Practice Research Scholarships and encouraged in the Beacon School policy as a means of schools in receipt of extra resourcing working with teachers in other schools on these skills. The schools in the University of Newcastle school-based research consortium funded by the Teacher Training Agency worked on development of thinking skills with encouraging results (for example, see McGrane, 2000).

Other examples of impact

Other areas in which research evidence has had an impact on policy and in some cases practice, include that on the evaluation of the national literacy and numeracy strategies, school governors, the provision of study support, the evaluation of the Beacon School policy, citizenship and the strategy for continuing professional development of teachers. Beyond schooling there are further examples, one being the strategy on adult skills. The Birth Cohort Study and International Adult Literacy Surveys provided important evidence of the impact on the rates of return to learning. This informed the national strategy for Adult Basic Skills.

3.15. Concluding comments

While progress is being made there is no justification for complacency. The "juries" of researchers, teachers, policy-makers and funders are still out on the progress made over the last five years. Some of the key issues that need to be addressed include:

- continuing to develop and make more transparent the criteria for judging quality across the range of methodologies in educational research;
- generating more high quality evidence capable of having an impact on policy and/or practice;
- providing more development opportunities in research methods;
- improving the access to currently available "best" evidence;
- establishing the support and involvement of many, if not most educational researchers to contribute to systematic reviews;
- securing long term resources for systematic reviewing;
- improving the capacity of policy-makers to access and use research;
- developing greater demand for, understanding of and opportunities to participate in research amongst practitioners;
- supporting the development of greater collaboration between higher education, local education authorities and schools on research which will contribute towards genuine user engagement.

This list involves culture changes at every level which are beginning to occur but have further to go. policy-makers need to "value" the role of evidence. Teachers need to look beyond their own schools for evidence. Funders need to make user engagement and planning for dissemination and impact requirements of research funding. Researchers need to be rewarded for appropriate achievements relating to impact in assessments of research.

Bibliography

Barber, M. (2001), Large-scale educational reform in England: work in progress. A paper for the school development conference, Tartu University, Estonia.

Black, P. and D. Wiliam (1998), *Inside the Black Box: raising standards through classroom assessment*, King's College, London.

Blunkett, D. (2000), *Influence or Irrelevance: can Social Science improve government?* Secretary of State's ESRC Lecture 2 February, DfEE, London.

Bynner, J., S. McIntosh, A. Vignoles, L. Dearden, H. Reed, and J. Van Reenen, (2001), *Improving Adult Basic Skills: Benefits to the individual and to society*, DfEE, London.

Dobson, J. and K. Henthorne (1999), *Pupil Mobility in Schools*, DfEE, London.

Dyson, A. and C. Desforges (2002), Building research capacity: some possible lines of action, A discussion paper for the National Educational Research Forum, *www.nerf-uk.org*.

Edwards, T. (2000), *Some reasonable expectations of educational research*. UCET Research Paper No 2, Universities Council for the Education for Teachers, London.

Fielding, M. (2002), Beyond the rhetoric of student voice: new departures or new constraints in the transformation of 21st century schooling? Paper presented to the AERA annual conference, April, 2002, New Orleans.

Furlong, J. (1998), *Educational Research: Meeting the challenge* Inaugural lecture, University of Bristol.

Furlong, J. and P. White (2002), *Educational Research Capacity in Wales* Cardiff: School of Social Sciences, Cardiff University.

Galton, M., J. Gray, and J. Rudduck (1999), *The Impact of School Transitions and Transfers on Pupil Progress and Attainment,*. DfEE, London.

Gray, J. (1998), The contribution of educational research to the cause of school improvement. Professorial lecture, Institute of Education, University of London, 29 April 1998.

Hargreaves, D. (1994), *The Mosaic of Learning: Schools and Teachers for the Next Century*, DEMOS, London.

Hargreaves, D. (1996) Teaching as a research-based profession: possibilities and prospects. *The Teacher Training Agency Annual Lecture 1996.*

Hargreaves, D. (1998), *Creative professionalism: the role of teachers in the knowledge society*, DEMOS, London.

Hillage, J., R. Pearson, A. Anderson, and P. Tamkin, (1998), *Excellence in Research on Schools*, DfEE London.

Kirkwood, M. (2002), Educational research in Scotland: policy context and key issues *Research Intelligence 79*, pp. 33-40.

McGrane, J. (2000), It's all in the mind, *Teachers*, DfEE, London.

McGuinness, C. (1999), *From Thinking Skills to Thinking Classrooms: A Review and Evaluation of Approaches for Developing Pupils' Thinking*, DfEE, London:

Mortimore, P. and J. Mortimore (1999), Does educational research influence policy or practice? In I. Abbott (ed.) *The Future of Education Research*, Falmer, London.

Raymond, L. (2001), Student involvement in school improvement: from data source to significant voice. *Forum* 43, pp. 58-61.

Rudduck, J. and D. McIntyre (eds.) (1998), *Challenges for Educational Research*, Paul Chapman, London.

Shavelson, R. and L. Towne (2001), *Scientific Inquiry in Education*, Report of the National Research Council, National Academy Press, Washington.

Tooley, J. and D. Darby (1998), "Educational Research – A Critique. A Survey of Published Educational Research", OFSTED (Office for Standards in Education), United Kingdom.

Wiliam, D. and C. Lee (2001), Teachers developing assessment for learning: impact on student achievement. Paper presented to the annual BERA conference, University of Leeds, September 2001.

ISBN 92-64-10030-X
New Challenges for Educational Research
© OECD 2003

PART II

New Zealand's Educational R&D System

ISBN 92-64-10030-X
New Challenges for Educational Research
© OECD 2003

PART II

Chapter 4

OECD Review of New Zealand's R&D System
Examiner's Report
October 2001

Abstract.   *This chapter present the OECD review of New Zealand's educational R&D system. New Zealand has a clear commitment to a strategic approach to educational R&D as a policy commitment with an open and evolving debate on education priorities involving policy-makers, researchers and practitioners. The review addresses a number of themes such as the scope, volume, themes and type of educational R&D, research capacity and the interface between research and practice and policy in New Zealand.*

4.1. Background to the review

This is the first OECD review of a member country's educational R&D policy. This report therefore combines two functions. It reviews the policy of a specific country, New Zealand, and comes to some specific conclusions in relation to that country; but it is also exploratory, in the sense that this initial exercise can be used to refine and develop the approach for future reviews in other countries. Many of the questions we raise in this report are, we suspect, common across most OECD countries – in particular the relationship between proper educational research and policy-making. We owe our New Zealand colleagues a debt of gratitude for being the first participants in this series of reviews, and their willingness to help in developing the field.

The preparatory work for the review identified four main themes to be covered:

- National policies and agenda for educational R&D.
- Organisation and funding of the educational R&D system.
- Outcomes of educational R&D in terms of teaching and learning, and policy-making.
- Strategies for producer-user interaction.

These provided a useful framework within which to conduct the review. We have not structured the report simply according to these themes as such, but we relate many of our comments specifically to them.

The review also links to a parallel OECD exercise around knowledge management.[1] In line with OECD's overall mission this addresses the issue of how policies to support knowledge-based economies can be developed. Amongst other things it strongly implies that educational policies, including those on R&D, need to be located within a broader context, with a particular concern for the way knowledge is generated, validated and utilised across sectors. We refer to this at several points in the report.

We wish to make one thing clear from the outset. We are very aware of the size of New Zealand. It is not a large country, and its human resources are inevitably thinly stretched. Our analysis and recommendations do take this into account. If our recommendations appear ambitious it is because in our judgement New Zealand both needs to make something of a quantum jump in its educational research policy, and is capable of it. We acknowledge that New Zealand has already begun to address these issues.

On UNESCO figures New Zealand has a very high fraction of its young people in post secondary education (63% in 1997), much higher than most European countries. The educational system as a whole is of good quality. At the same time, New Zealand invests far less in R&D of any kind than other developed countries, and has far fewer R&D personnel per million population than Australia and Western European countries. In other words, New Zealand is successful educationally, but is, by R&D standards, not becoming a knowledge economy.

In our brief (5-day) visit we spoke to a wide range of stakeholders : policy-makers in several different ministries; researchers in different roles from a number of institutions; union representatives; advisory body members; teachers from a primary school and a teacher college; a list is included in Appendix 4.1. Inevitably there were others with whom it would have been useful to speak, but time was lacking. This report is therefore a synoptic view, and not in any sense a comprehensive analysis.

4.2. The New Zealand context

At a general level, New Zealand has a number of distinctive features, which shape its position on R&D.

Size and location

New Zealand is a small country, with a population of less than 4 million. It has a well-developed education system, which has expanded and changed rapidly over the last decade, but its size places inevitable constraints on the volume and types of R&D which can be expected or aspired to. This is a matter of economic capacity but also of human resources; there simply cannot be enough researchers to cover even all the high research priorities in depth. The size factor is compounded by the country's geographical isolation. Even in these days of global instant communication, the fact that New Zealand is three hours flying time from the nearest neighbour inevitably reduces the level of natural interchange of information, ideas and people. New Zealand is therefore in a very different position from, say, a comparably-sized European country such as Denmark.

Economic structure

New Zealand has historically been, and remains, an economy which is heavily dependent on primary production. Its service sector is well developed, but it has never had a significant industrial sector. The country's R&D capacity has certainly been affected by this, since it has not been able to draw on the dynamism supplied elsewhere by industrial change and innovation. In quantitative terms, R&D expenditure as a percentage of GDP in New Zealand reached 1.1% in 1997/98, which is low by OECD standards, and only 30% of all funds spent on R&D comes from the private sector.[2] Analysing the implications of this would go well beyond the scope of this report, but it constitutes a relevant background feature.

Political and cultural change

Over the last decade and more, New Zealand has engaged in political changes, which have had a major impact on the values and procedures characterising policy-making and practice. Central here has been the shift away from a society with a secure welfare foundation towards a strongly market-oriented system. These changes have been particularly evident in education. These are not matters of technical policy; they go to the heart of New Zealand society. The changes, *e.g.* the move to self-managing schools or competitive recruitment in higher education, appear to have been mainly driven by political conviction rather than evidence-based analysis; moreover they do not appear to have been accompanied by systematic evaluation of their impact. The emphasis on market solutions has made it harder to establish clear research priorities. Debate on future directions and the appropriate role of marked systems is now opening up, which makes this review timely. Developing a tradition of research-based policy will take time.

Against this background, we see clear signs of a commitment to a strategic approach to educational R&D as a policy commitment. We have a strong sense of an evolving debate on educational priorities, and of a desire that this debate should be an open and inclusive one, involving policy-makers, researchers and practitioners. A major goal of this report is to give support and further impetus to this emerging trend.

The most direct evidence of this commitment (apart from the Ministry's willingness to participate in this review) is the Statement of Strategic Research Priorities: Directions and Opportunities. Here two strategic policy priorities are identified:

● Reducing underachievement.

● Promoting excellence.

A foundation for developing the strategic approach has been laid with the commissioning of nine broad literature reviews (see Appendix 4.2). The range encompassed is impressive, and provides a major input into any debate on future strategic directions. The process of commissioning is itself significant, since it involved drawing on international as well as domestic expertise a laudable recognition of the need to make use of external research capacity.

The literature reviews have led on to a hierarchical structure for future educational research priorities, with three levels. The top level is comprised of

---

Box 4.1.   **Future educational research priorities – level one**

Theme 1: Addressing Underachievement

Focus Areas:

Early Foundation

Raising Achievement

Working with Diversity

Tertiary Participation and Achievement

Theme 2 : Building Professional Capacity

Focus Areas :

Stocktaking capability

Developing the Learning Profession

Theme 3: Education for Economic and Social Achievement

Focus Areas:

Community Development

Lifelong Learning

---

three *themes:* Addressing Underachievement; Building Professional Capacity; and Education for Economic and Social Achievement. Each theme is then broken down in to *Focus Areas,* and then *Strands.* It is worth reproducing this framework in outline (at the first two levels), in order to promote consistency in the debate since the more that it is publicly available the more that stakeholders will have a common focus for their discussions but also to enable identification of major gaps, which we shall contribute to in this report. As the work on these priorities is currently in progress, the final priorities might change.

The framework is rightly broad in its coverage. A comprehensive review would use it to map and evaluate existing research, in order to reach conclusions about the current state of play. Ours is a much more synoptic approach. What we can say at this stage is this (the following three comments can be taken into account as the work on the strategic priorities is still in progress):

● There are some particularly obvious gaps, notably in post-compulsory education and lifelong learning even though these figure in the themes.

● There is a need for communication and collaboration (though not necessarily co-ordination), both within the education sector and between the education and other sectors.

- The framework does not of itself generate the prioritisation required to give a strategic perspective; it will require active intersectoral dialogue and political support to achieve this.

4.3. Scope and definition

The first issue which the review threw up was the definition of the field. There are several aspects to this:

- What counts as "research," and how does this link to "development?"
- What is accepted as falling under the heading "education?"
- How far is there consensus on this, and how is debate formulated?
- How do the policy and funding structures reflect this understanding?

These are issues, which would be applicable in most countries. The original OECD exercise which led to these reviews wrestled with definitional issues at some length.[3] In New Zealand they have specific salience.

On the first issue, we can map research against a hierarchy which leads from data to facts to knowledge to understanding (and then, sometimes, to wisdom). Data is important, whether quantitative or qualitative, and we have more to say about this below. But the use to which data is put, and then the reflection on it, is crucial if we are to talk convincingly of a "knowledge society". In other words, a knowledge society is not one which has accumulated mountains of facts, but one which knows how to sort them, make sense of them and act upon the sense it makes. A significant issue for us is how far the very substantial amounts of data being collected are effectively used. This is especially important given the difficulty of developing policies, which are based effectively on evidence and knowledge. We acknowledge that some progress has been made with the Education Indicators Framework, which has been created around three focus areas (early foundations, ready to participate and lifelong learning). This Framework utilises quantitative and qualitative data from a wide range of sources that includes international and national system wide assessments and research and evaluation projects.

Similarly, how do we divide "research" from "development"? The very phrase "R&D" suggests a close link, even an umbilical one. But the relationship may not be simple. In our view the overall picture of R&D in New Zealand is skewed towards the "D" in ways which may disguise some research weaknesses.

The issue is one of balance. Within the overall effort put into "research", is there an appropriate balance between fact- and statistic-gathering and the analysis and use of those data? In our view, there is some doubt as to whether the distinction (fuzzy though it is) is always appreciated in New Zealand. This has implications both for the kinds of research commissioned, and for the use made of the data. The R/D relationship poses a similar question of balance; in our view much of what appears to come under the heading "research" is in fact development work, notably on assessment. This is not a question of being purist about research, and certainly not about ranking one activity above another; it is of clarifying the overall picture. Having noted this, we do acknowledge that there are efforts being made to address this issue, for example, the Strategic Research Initiative and the Education Indicators Framework.

There is a further aspect, of particular significance to New Zealand. We heard of the distinctive Maori approach to knowledge generally and therefore to research. As we understand it (and this necessarily oversimplifies) this places great emphasis on the collective development, validation and use of knowledge, and on action-oriented modes of executing research. These are distinguished from individualised approaches to research, with weaker links to specific communities. This distinction could lead us into areas of deep epistemological debate, with a real possibility of fundamentally different paradigms. Here all we can do is encourage the strengthening and continuation an active and practical debate on different conceptions of research – including but not restricted to the Maori-Pakeha dimension – so that there can be a common understanding of different positions. This debate should be led from within the research community.[4]

A further question concerns the extent to which "education" refers only to what goes in the formal education system. We were impressed to read in the report. We endorse the view, well expressed in the initial report of the Tertiary Education Advisory Commission (Shaping the Vision, p. 9), that much learning occurs beyond the boundaries of formal providers, with significant implications for policy and research. It raises, though, difficulties when it comes even to producing an inventory of relevant research, once the boundaries of the formal system are breached. But in any case we saw amongst practitioners and policy-makers a conception of educational research which focuses heavily on the formal education system, and especially on schools. Research activity appears to be highly segmented even within the educational system, with little activity spanning school and post-school sectors and little awareness of activity in other sectors. We would encourage a broadening of the overall focus, and a stronger sense of the overall educational system.

4.4. Volume

It is worth going back to the 1990 communiqué from OECD Ministers of Education, which can be seen as the origin of this whole exercise:

"In general, the level of investment in research and development in education and training is far lower than in any other sector of comparable size. The potential or educational research as an integral element of improvement remains largely underdeveloped, whether at national, regional or local level."

(OECD 1992 p. 35, quoted in OECD 1995 p. 8). The position may have changed somewhat over the past decade, but it is unlikely to have been transformed in most OECD countries. So there is a general picture of low capacity. Against that, however, New Zealand still appears to be lagging.

In OECD (1995), there is a 1991-92 estimation of educational R&D spending in New Zealand of NZD 7 million corresponding to 95 full-time equivalent researchers (working full-time on research). These figures most likely underestimate today's educational R&D effort in New Zealand as we shall see in the following attempt to estimate its volume.

Assessing how much educational research is taking place is not easy, even if one confines it to research on the formal education system. This is partly because of the distinction between research and development, where we felt that the apparent amount of research was somewhat inflated by the inclusion of very substantial (and effective) development projects to do with assessment. But there are other problems, even within a small country's system.

Table 4.1 was helpfully supplied to us by the Ministry of Education, and identifies the main key components of the Ministry spending on educational R&D from the 1st July 1997 to the 30th June 2001.

Table 4.1. **Expenditure on educational R&D 1 July 1997-30 June 2001 (New Zealand Ministry of Education)**

Source of funding	NZD
Budget appropriations	16 500 000
Budget appropriations for specific programmes and or policies	(2 300 000)
Assessment pool – reviews, R&D and evaluations	(3 200 000)
Assessment Resource Banks	(4 000 000)
National Education Monitoring Project	(7 000 000)
Funding from Research Division Operations	3 600 000
Funding from other Division Operations	1 200 000
Other (includes external funds and inter-agency)	200 000
Total	**21 500 000**

In addition to these quantitative figures in Table 4.1, which only take into account the Ministry of Education's funding of R&D programmes, we would like to add the following points:

● The Ministry of Education's own operational research programme, amounting this to some NZD 1.1 million. This funds a series of projects tied to the Ministry's own priorities.

● Appropriations, from Vote Education or other Votes (*i.e.* government budget headings), amount to significantly more. Dominant here is the National

Education Monitoring Project (NEMP), a well-regarded means of feeding back to teachers in the classroom information on assessment outcomes. The allocation to NEMP is of the order of NZD 7 million. Combined with the NZD 4 million allocations to the Assessment Resource Banks (ARBs) this represents a significant funding commitment, far outstripping the defined research component.

- Allocation to the New Zealand Council for Educational Research. NZCER receives a core grant from the Ministry of Education of NZD 1.43 million, which it matches with income from other sources, mainly consultancy and publications.

- General research activity carried out within tertiary institutions. This is the most difficult area to assess. One would expect academic staff, especially those in Schools or Departments of Education within universities, to be carrying out relevant research. Public funding for tertiary institutions contains an element for research, especially at postgraduate level where funded EFTS places increased by 82% between 1992 and 1999 to over 14 000, almost all of it in universities. However the research funding component of the EFTS funding is not separately identified. The Ministry of Research, Science and Technology estimates the total inbuilt funding for university research to be in the order of NZD 140 million per year.

A very crude estimate for this input side in relation to educational R&D could be made by estimating how many staff work in Education departments, taking an average salary, and applying 20% as a notional time allocation for research (recognising that this will vary widely within and across institutions). However we believe this would not give a true indication of the volume of activity. Partly this is because not all institutions, or Schools of Education, insist on research. One estimate put the proportion of staff so engaged at around 25%, and it is the case elsewhere that university academics working in education are commonly less research-oriented than most. But partly it is because the increase in student numbers coupled with a decline in the unit of resource per student over the last decade has limited the time available for research. Staff do not have the time to carry out substantial research, especially where they are involved in a major field of professional training. Getting a clearer picture of the level of activity in this sphere is important.

There are other components, which are outside Vote Education:

- *Marsden Fund.* This is a substantial fund, some NZD 26 million annually, which gives awards for blue sky research, mainly to academics. However, competition is intense, with less than 10% of rated proposals being funded; social science in general gets very little of these [only around 7 %] The Royal Society of New Zealand's Strategic Report 2000 confirms this picture. Within that education does very poorly, so that we are aware of only a single

Marsden award going for educational research. As in other respects there is a vicious circle at work here, with the minimal access to Marsden funding preventing the building-up of this kind of research capacity.

- *Public Good Science Fund.* This fund in fact no longer exists discretely but is distributed over a number of areas as a general part of the Morst Vote. For the purposes of this report we can still refer to it, however, and note that it has increased very substantially, from NZD 1 million in 1996/7 to NZD 25.8 million in 2000/01 (RSNZ report p. 5). Yet from the point of view of educational research it has only funded very few such projects.

- *Health Research Council.* Health has significant overlaps with education in policy and research. The overall budget for health research is substantial, at NZD 33 million, and the HRC was commended to us as a possible model for education, notably in its recognition of specific Maori issues.

- The Ministry of Research Science and Technology has other budget headings potentially relevant to education, notably one of NZD 4.3 million on Social Research. However we are not aware of any of this being devoted to educational issues, nor to research which is not educational but which is related to education. Also to be noted is the specific category of Maori Knowledge and Development increased in 2000/01 to NZD 4 million.

Based on all the different funding sources available for educational R&D in New Zealand a very rough estimate of today's educational R&D expenditure is NZD 12-14 million. Comparisons with other countries are difficult. However, OECD (1995) gives some indications. The level of the educational R&D as a percentage of total expenditure on education is on average 0.3% in seven OECD countries for which data is available (Australia, Canada, Finland, Ireland, Netherlands, Sweden, and United Kingdom). In England, the recent figure is 0.5%. Given that the total expenditure on education in New Zealand is around NZD 7.1 billion, the educational R&D as a percentage of total expenditure on education is around 0.17-0.20 %. In summary we would say that the OECD's figures show New Zealand as having a relatively low expenditure on R&D generally, and the figures shown above suggest strongly that within this relatively low figure social science, and within social science education, do relatively poorly. Overall, therefore, we have to conclude that in straight volume terms the country cannot claim a strong commitment to educational research.

4.5. Distribution

Mode

One conventional categorisation divides research into basic or blue sky; strategic and applied. Basic research is not tied to any specific practical goals, but is undertaken primarily to acquire new knowledge of underlying phenomena. It is largely curiosity driven. It may of course have immediate policy or practical applications, but these are not part of its design. The Marsden fund and infrastructural funding for universities are intended to support this kind of research. We saw very little sign of this in the educational field.

Strategic research operates between basic and applied, with a longer time horizon and broader goals than the latter. We saw evident signs that New Zealand aspires to develop a strategic approach to research. The commissioning of reviews of research covering eight domains is a promising start; the test will come as the implications of these reviews are worked through. However a strategic approach to research should be distinguished from research which is itself strategic; the former does not necessarily imply a strong commitment to the kinds of longer-term, cumulative work which characterises the latter. So a long- or medium-term goal such as enhancing social and economic performance needs to be supported by research which is itself longer-term, as well as by projects with a more immediate focus.

Applied research is defined as original investigation directed primarily towards a specific practical aim or objective. Evaluation studies are a prime example of this. Our impression is that the great bulk of educational research in New Zealand is concentrated at the applied end, and particularly on assessment issues where we were made aware of an impressive array of instruments with good links to practice. This is not to downplay the value of these, and the overall intention to establish a "culture of evaluation" is perfectly valid in order to use these evaluations to change things, i.e. with feedback loops leading to action. The point we are making here is that the balance between different types of research is a salient issue for R&D policy.

Institutional

New Zealand has recently created a "level playing field" in the funding of tertiary institutions. All institutions which are recognised as providing higher education receive the same amount for a given student in a given subject area at a given level. Little seems to be known of the impact of the new funding system on academic research generally, and educational research in particular. Those institutions which provide postgraduate education – overwhelmingly the universities – receive a higher proportion of higher-level EFTS funding, since postgraduate teaching is more research-based. However the expectation is that all degree-level teaching is in some measure research-based. This raises the questions of how far the creation of a unitary tertiary sector has entailed a dilution of research, since the entry of many new institutions means that resources are more thinly spread. This is indeed a strong *a priori* line of argument, and we have more to say below on the issue of critical mass. However we also heard – and not only from the Colleges themselves – that Colleges of Education were doing applied research which was of direct classroom application, and also encouraging teachers themselves to engage in small-scale research.

In a sense, therefore, we may be seeing the growth of more applied forms of research but a lack of concentrated strategic or basic research. This dilemma could only be resolved by an overall increase in funding.

4.6. Contract culture

As part of the general shift towards a more market-oriented society, the last decade has seen a major change in the procedures and formulae for funding education generally and educational research in particular. This has led in turn to a change in the sector's culture, with competition for contracts becoming far more pronounced. We could not ourselves judge the impact of the shift, but clearly most practitioners felt that the extent of it had been largely detrimental.

We feel it necessary to distinguish several different – components: institutional competition for students; competition among researchers for research funding; and the nature of the research contracts awarded. The former is a crucial contextual factor. University funding is dominated by student recruitment, where money follows the student and EFTS is the major source of university income.[5] Even in an expanding market (total EFTS-based funding increased by 18.8% between 1991 and 1999), this has strong features of a zero-sum game, where one institution benefits mainly at the expense of another. It has led to a high degree of competition between institutions, with few geographical boundaries limiting the competition. The competition has been accentuated by the decline in EFTS funding. This has been estimated at 33% between 1980 and 1998 (Scott and Scott 2000, p. 6), with an accompanying rise in the EFTS to staff ratio of 48%, from 12.5 to 18.4. This has had two major relevant impacts: it has significantly affected the time generally available to academics for research; and it has sharpened competition between institutions.

The former factor – time – has an obvious direct negative impact on research activity. But competition for students need not necessarily directly affect the second element identified above, namely collaborative relationships between researchers. However we found evidence of institutions becoming so imbued with the competitive spirit that they discouraged or even debarred their members from collaborating on research with colleagues from other institutions. This obviously has an overall negative effect, especially in a limited pool.

We would emphasise that competition and collaboration are not polar opposites. In many contexts, including industrial ones, competition actively fosters collaboration, providing more incentives for people to get together to design or execute research. It is a question of the overall levels of energy in the system, and the norms, which govern the process. There is scope here for procedures for commissioning research to be reviewed, but also for institutional leaders to review their own practices.

A separate issue concerns the nature of the contracts issued. Here we refer mainly to the Ministry of Education's commissioned research. This is important not so much because of its absolute volume, but because of its preponderance in the contract research field. We were struck by the extent to which the Ministry dominance of research project funding. Naturally, and appropriately, the Ministry's research concerns tend towards the applied end, and to have a relatively short-term focus reflecting political priorities. This is not a problem when there is a wider set of research funders, but in New Zealand this is not the case. There is no autonomous research council, and very few foundations (if any) ready to provide resources for educational research. (The Wolf-Fischer Trust's support for Maori education appears to be an exception). Whilst some researchers are clearly successful in putting together a running series of research projects with Ministry funding, the short-term contractual nature of most of the work almost certainly increases fragmentation. It will also inhibit the ability to build capacity within the research community: the development of research expertise and experience, but also the ability to look beyond applied research topics and frame research questions in a longer-term context.

The emergence of a competitive contract culture has a wider significance. Increasingly, policy-makers and researchers are interested in the notion of social capital as a complement to human capital. Social capital is to be found in the networks and relationships, which foster trust and reciprocity towards mutual ends. The general line of argument is that individual skills and competences will only make their full contribution to a knowledge society if they are located within a functional set of social relationships (OECD, 2001). This applies as much to educational research as to other fields; it would be deeply ironic if educational research showed declining social capital in its efforts to build human capital.

4.7. Coverage

The framework of Themes and Focus Areas in educational R&D outlined above presents a formidable challenge. Moreover educational research can cover a huge range of topics; it can also draw on a wide range of disciplines. Even large countries have difficulties in encompassing the research possibilities generated by the challenge of developing a knowledge-based society. Nevertheless there appear to us to be some significant gaps in the coverage of New Zealand research.

By far the most evident is in research beyond schooling. At the schools level New Zealand covers a reasonable range of research topics, though whether these have a sufficiently broad disciplinary base may be questionable. Tertiary education is far less well covered. We are aware of some studies, for example of rates of return to university study, and of participation. But given the dramatic expansion of post-secondary education we are struck by the paucity of research on the impact of this on social chances, on the character of university provision and on its labour market implications. Moreover the broader field of lifelong learning – community and adult education, training and organisational development – appears to be largely undeveloped. Arguably, activity in this latter field is largely confined to work, which concerns the Maori community, with its emphasis on collective learning. The fact that lifelong learning is not a research priority may indeed be restricting opportunities for Maori researchers.

There is a growing recognition in New Zealand of the significance of lifelong learning. In his foreword to the TEAC's second report, *Shaping the System*, the Associate Minister of Education Steve Maharey registers a commitment to a broad and inclusive vision of lifelong learning, and to placing tertiary education at the heart of the drive for a knowledge society. There are two dimensions to this, and research is lacking in both of them. One is the distribution of educational opportunities over the life course in relation to the formal education system – in other words, patterns of participation which extend beyond the entry into tertiary education of young people from the school system. The second is the incidence and significance of learning beyond formal education, in economic organisations and in communities.

This raises the issue of intersectoral relationships and communication. In a small country, one might expect such communication to be relatively developed, since the members of a relatively small body of researchers and policy-makers will naturally know each other to a greater extent than in a country with a large population. We are not convinced that this advantage is properly exploited. It may also, as was pointed out to us, be a constraint, where people know each other too closely and are therefore unwilling to take risks or break ranks. The broad framework which is beginning to emerge allows these possibilities to be explored in future.

This is not only a question of knowing what is going on in other policy areas. A key issue for research is the interaction between policy and practice in different spheres, for example between education and the labour market, or between education and health. We understand that there have been attempts in the past to fashion a common agenda in the former area, but that this did not lead to positive outcomes.

As we have said, it would be wholly unreasonable to expect New Zealand researchers to cover the full gamut of research areas. Nevertheless we are clear that the current distribution is not well geared to meeting the challenges of a learning society. More work on tertiary education and lifelong learning generally is an obvious priority; and serious thought should be given to how to include wider socio-demographic issues, for instance the implications of changing proportions of Maori and Pacific Island people in the New Zealand population, or the consequences of population ageing for teaching professions at all levels.

4.8. Research capacity

Training

A recent exercise on mapping educational research capacity and capability was undertaken by Professor Brian Findsen of Auckland University of Technology. The Ministry of Education commissioned this work. The full results from this will be a welcome addition to the picture of educational R&D. The report points to the diversity of capacity, which exists, with distinctive forms of research capacity within different institutional types. The single tertiary sector which now exists, with all tertiary institutions funded on a similar basis, nevertheless encompasses distinctive groupings of research focus. Thus as one would expect the older universities have a stronger focus on basic research, whilst colleges of education are much more concerned with applied forms of research, with close links to practitioners.

The Findsen report covers trends which impact on research careers. In particular it identifies the ways in which professional development is assuming a more central role in advanced qualifications. This affects both the content of what is researched, and the mode. Part-time routes to graduate qualifications allow closer integration of research and practice, but limit the extent to which a full range of sophisticated research techniques and experience can be acquired. The growth of the professional development mode means on the one hand that more teachers are developing contact with research, both executing research themselves and becoming more closely acquainted with research processes and results. On the other hand, it means that educational research as a career is not a strongly defined pathway.

Once again this is a question of balance. The integration of research and classroom practice is clearly a positive. At the same time, the capacity base needs to be safeguarded and nurtured, so that there is a sufficiency of researchers with the skills and commitment to sustain a research community. Postgraduate qualifications in educational research are not the only means to achieve this, but they are likely to be central to a successful long-term research capability. There are concerns about the quality of the graduate training programme, accentuated by the demise of the Research Affiliate Programme which used to provide a limited number of teachers with fulltime leave for research.

Expertise

There is a further very important aspect to this, which brings us back to the question of what constitutes research. We do not conclude that New Zealand is particularly lacking in the accumulation of data, given its size. Arguably, indeed, there is too much data to be satisfactorily handled; for example the accumulation of data on children in relation to school accountability seems to have reached saturation levels [evidence from Strengthening Education in Bangere and Otara Evaluation (SEMO)]. But we do think that there is little capacity for exploiting the data, which exists to anything like its full potential. We suspect that there is something of a vicious circle at work here. There is relatively little capacity, even amongst established academic researchers, for exploring datasets systematically.

This means that future generations of researchers have little chance of developing such expertise, and the opportunity for cumulative analysis and debate does not exist. Thus it is not so much a question of suggesting that large numbers of new datasets are needed, as of building the capacity to exploit existing data to a level of reasonable sophistication.

Part of this concerns the integration of different datasets. For example, we heard that labour market datasets held by Skills NZ are not related to educational datasets. We should stress that these kinds of issue are not unique to New Zealand; by and large, compatibility of datasets and their effective utilisation are usually a problem in any country. But the lack of sophisticated analytical expertise accentuates the problem in relation to educational research and debate in New Zealand.

Capacity and culture are interrelated. We detected some signs of a bias, which is to be found in other countries also, of disinclination on the part of educational researchers to engage in quantitative research generally, and for quantitative evidence to figure strongly in debates within educational circles. This flags up issues, which derive from the relative isolation of educational R&D from other fields and disciplines.

Intermediary capacity

This leads to the question of whether there should be an intermediary body between researchers and government. We have already commented on the unusual extent to which the Ministry of Education is directly involved in forming the research agenda and in commissioning research, and the way this is likely to influence content and approach. In the feedback sessions towards the end of our visit we offered the view that for reasons of size a separate fully-fledged commissioning body for educational research was not a realistic prospect. This was challenged by some members of the research community present, yet our view is that such a body would be likely to absorb precious research capacity in relatively unproductive forms of work –

in other words, in organisational activity rather than actual research output. The volume of educational research is simply not sufficient to justify a separate intermediary body.

However, we do see a need for a mechanism, which would allow research programmes to be developed which are not directly sourced from the Ministry of Education. This is important in order both to provide a more diverse base for research than currently exists, and to provide different models for commissioning and evaluating research. There seem to us to be two possible ways forward. One is to set up a semi-autonomous research council, but one which embraced the social sciences generally, within which education would play a part. This higher level of aggregation would allow an appropriate economy of scale. It would also have the advantage of bringing education into a closer relationship with other social sciences. The other is to develop a less institutionalised but still significant form of intermediation, such as a consultative group of researchers (from universities, NZCER and elsewhere) and other stakeholders and other disciplines, which would develop research priorities, advise on their implementation and support, and comment on progress and achievement.

Concentration/critical mass

All of these reinforce the case, which has already been made in more than one report, for a greater concentration of research expertise. New Zealand now has a huge number of tertiary institutions, all of which at least in principle can be engaged in research. Most obviously, there are upwards of 50 colleges of education, each of which might be claiming to do research (though only a small proportion do to any recognisable extent). We recognise that the inclusion of all such institutions in a single sector has enhanced the capacity of the sector to carry out applied work, and strengthened the links between research and practice.[6] However it is clear to us that there is a trade-off between diffusion and the capacity to carry out basic and long-term research....here is a serious need to find ways of clustering research expertise.

We endorse the recommendation of the Tertiary Education Advisory Committee's report, *Shaping the System*: "The system must be designed to promote and sustain world-class research capacity and capability, including that of Maori and Pacific peoples. This will require greater specialisation and concentration of research activity within the tertiary education system. The Commission recommends the establishment or recognition of national centres or networks of research excellence within the tertiary education system, with linkages to a national strategy and the international research community. They will also need strong linkages with other parts of the tertiary education system and with those outside it."

We particularly endorse the need to think in terms of networks as well as centres. We understand that there might be a case in some areas for concentrating researchers within a single institution. But this is not the only way forward. Turning New Zealand's size to advantage and using new ICT, there is considerable scope for developing mechanisms, which allow intellectual concentration without physical juxtaposition.

Such networks and centres need not necessarily map directly to the themes of focal areas specified in the strategic framework. They should take account of current capacity in the field, and of the ambitions of active researchers (given especially that intrinsic curiosity on the part of researchers is one of the stronger guarantees of research quality). The kinds of issues to be addressed in developing them include:

● the process of identifying the key topics/themes around which they are to be built;

● the opportunity to broaden the disciplinary base of educational research, ensuring that researchers from outside mainstream education departments are involved;

● the integration of a capacity-building function into their activities, *e.g.* through graduate training programmes;

● a commitment to a common approach to exploring and exploiting national datasets.

It would, finally, be a great step forward if at least some of these centres/networks were supported out of Votes other than the Education Vote, such as Labour, Health.

4.9. Interface with practice and policy

We found that overall the quality of communication between research and practice is high. This is most true at the schools level, not surprisingly given the focus of research on the school system. There are three aspects to this. First, dissemination is well handled. In particular, publications such as "SET – Research Information for Teachers" make results available in an easily accessible way, such that teachers with little time for research reading can become aware of them, and school principals can develop a good overview of research relevant to their schools. Secondly, as we have already mentioned, many teachers are undertaking professional upgrading which includes a research component. This brings them into contact with research, and may even involve them in conducting research themselves, leading to a greater sensitivity on their part to the value as well as the vocabulary of research.

Thirdly, there have been some interesting developments in the form of participatory research activities, linking researchers with practitioners. The most prominent example of this, which to our benefit we were able to visit, is the SEMO project addressing the problems of an underachieving area in South Auckland. Here it is evident that a process of dialogue had been established over priorities and procedures, involving principals, teachers, the parents and their representatives and the researchers. The project is clearly well placed to shape policy-making. Not all research can be designed in this way, obviously, and the expectations of practitioners about the accessibility and immediate relevance of research are not always realistic; but examples such as this can do much to promote productive communication.

There was much less evidence of active interface between research and practice at other levels, and especially between research and policy at all levels of the education system. Changes in the tertiary system appear to have been brought about without reference to research evidence and without even serious commitment to evaluation or analysis after the event. We saw little sign of research influencing teaching and learning within the university system. Given the apparent lack of research beyond the formal education system, there is *a fortiori* little significant impact on policy or practice in adult education or lifelong learning more generally.

Developing a tradition of evidence-based policy-making is a major challenge.[7] It entails longish-term commitments by both policy-makers and researchers, and complex and sophisticated arrangements for developing and evaluating evidence. One important distinction we would wish to stress is that it differs substantially from the kinds of project evaluation which may be relevant and important but which do not themselves constitute policy analysis.

4.10. Conclusions and recommendations

- We applaud recent moves to develop a strong and strategic approach to educational research in New Zealand. These foundations should be built on by promoting a wider debate on research priorities – substantive and in respect of research capacity.

- Significant progress will require additional resources. This should not be seen simply as expanding the system in its current form.

- We believe an expansion may best be seen as part of an overall expansion of funding for social sciences. Amongst other things, this should promote interaction between educational researchers and those from other disciplines.

- Resources also need to come from more diverse sources. There is at present overdependence on government, and especially on the Ministry of Education.

- There is scope for intermediation between the government and the research community. A Social Sciences Research Council, with a sub-group on educational research, could mark a significant step forward. A discrete educational research council is not a realistic option.

- The emerging framework of Themes and Focus Areas is promising. It reveals large research gaps in certain areas, notably in tertiary education and lifelong learning. Lifelong learning in particular includes community forms of learning, with special salience for the Maori community.

- A broader view of educational research means reviewing the links between research in different policy areas, notably with labour market, health and Maori/Pacific Island affairs.

- Attention needs to be paid to building up research capacity and infrastructure, as distinct from the commissioning of additional research. This is essential if medium- and longer-term R&D performance is to improve.

- Some concentration of research capacity is necessary. This need not mean physical concentration, but the explicit development of critical research masses around certain themes or fields.

- We do not think that competition and collaboration are necessarily in conflict. But we do see a need to shape the process of research formulation and execution so that it enhances rather than undermines social capital.

- Special attention should be paid to developing the capacity to make effective use of existing databases. This entails a significant exercise in staff development for existing as well as future researchers, and for policy-makers charged with managing research.

- Incentives could be useful in promoting research across disciplines, fields and sectors.

- The issue of building a tradition of evidence-based policy-making in education should be explicitly addressed.

Notes

1. See OECD (2000), "Knowledge Management in the Learning Society", Paris.

2. New Zealand Ministry of Research, Science and Technology: "New Zealand R&D Statistics 1997/98."

3. The eventual operational definition arrived at reads as follows:
"Educational R&D is systematic, original investigation or inquiry and associated development activities concerning the social, cultural, economic and political contexts within which educational systems operate and learning takes place; the purposes of education; the processes of teaching, learning and personal development of children, youth and adults; the work of educators; the resources and organisational arrangements to support educational work; the policies and strategies to achieve educational objectives; and the social, cultural, political and

economic outcomes of education." OECD (1995), *"Educational Research and Development: Trends, Issues and Challenges"*, Paris.

4. Blampied (2000) argues that a broader understanding of "scholarship" and its relation to research would also help give esteem to activities which serve Maori communities such as iwi history and community development.

5. In 1999 the EFTS Bulk Funding System was replaced by the Universal Tertiary Tuition Allowance, with no capping of places.

6. We understand, for example, that some of the smaller colleges which have entered the sector quite recently have been particularly relevant to the concerns of the Maori community, partly because their small size means that they can be closely related to very local communities.

7. As with many other observations in this report, this should not be construed as implying that other countries are notably more successful in this. In the UK, for example, the former Department of Education and Science was once described by its Permanent Secretary as a "knowledge-free zone". A specific Centre for Evidence-based Policy and Practice has now been established.

Bibliography

Blampied, N. (2000), "Scholarship : Its Nature and Significance for New Zealand Higher Education", Department of Psychology, University of Canterbury, Christchurch, New Zealand.

Ministry of Education (1999), "Strengthening Education in Mangere and Otara Education", First Evaluation Report, Research Division, Ministry of Education.

Ministry of Education (2000), "Statement of Strategic Research Priorities : Directions and Opportunities", Wellington, New Zealand.

Ministry of Education (2000), "New Zealand's Tertiary Education Sector : Profile and Trends", Wellington, New Zealand.

Ministry of Education (2001), "OECD Review of New Zealand's Educational Research and Development Systems", Background Report, Wellington, New Zealand.

Ministry of Research, Science and Technology (1998), "Building Tomorrow's Success – Guidelines for Thinking Beyond Today", Wellington, New Zealand.

Ministry of Research, Science and Technology (2000), "Transforming New Zealand : Challenges and opportunities in research, science and technology", Wellington, New Zealand.

OECD (1995), "Educational Research and Development – Trends Issues and Challenges", Paris.

OECD (1996), "Knowledge Bases for Educational Policies", Paris.

OECD (2000), "Knowledge Management in Learning Societies", Paris.

OECD (2001), "The Well-being of Nations : The Role of Human and Social Capital", Paris.

Scott and Scott (2000), "New Zealand University Funding over the Last Two Decades", The New Zealand Vice-Chancellors' Committee, Wellington.

Tertiary Education Advisory Commission (2001), "Shaping the System", 2nd Report, Wellington, New Zealand.

APPENDIX 4.1

Interviewed persons

Sandi Aiken	NZEI (Primary Teachers' Union)
Robin Baker	Director New Zealand Council for Educational Research
Dr. Neville Blampied	Association of University Staff
Elisabeth Eppel	Group Manager Ministry of Education
Howard Fancy	Chief Executive Ministry of Education
Dr. Alison Gilmore	Education Department University of Canterbury (President: New Zealand Association of Researchers in Education)
Professor John Hattie	School of Education University of Auckland
Margaret Ledgerton	Association of University Teachers
Gavin Lockwood	Manager Education Section The Treasury
Hon. Steve Maharey	Associate Minister of Education (Tertiary Education)
Rob McIntosh	Group Manager Ministry of Education
Dr. Lindsay Parry	Associate Principal Christchurch College of Education
Dr. Paul Reynolds	Chief Policy Analyst Ministry of Research Science and Technology
Professor Graham Smith	International Research Institute for Maori and Indigenous people University of Auckland

Associate Professor Lucie Smith	International Research Institute for Maori and Indigenous people University of Auckland
Amanda Torr	Manager Tertiary Education Advisory Committee (TEAC)
Lynne Whitney	Research Director Ministry of Education
Cathy Wylie	Senior Researcher New Zealand Council for Educational Research

Visit to primary school in South Auckland Strengthening Education in Mangere and Otara Evaluation (SEMO-project)

Kerrie Crossman	Yendarra School
Glenda Kitney	Yendarra School
Joan Simpson	Yendarra School
Colleen Murray	Yendarra School

APPENDIX 4.2

"State-of-the-art" Literature reviews commissioned by the Ministry of Education in New Zealand

● *The impact of family and community resources on student outcomes: an assessment of the international literature with implications for New Zealand.* Stanford University.

● *Early childhood education literature review.* Children's Issues Centre. Otago University.

● *The effects of curriculum and assessment on pedagogical approaches and on education outcomes.* University of Waikato.

● *Influence of peer effects on learning outcomes: a review of the literature.* University of Auckland.

● *Literature review of the effects of school resourcing on educational outcomes.* BERL/ Infometrics.

● *The effects of school governance, ownership, organisation and management on educational outcomes.* John Rentoul and John Rosanowski, with Dempster N, Fisher D, Hosking N, Hunter R, Pugh G and Walford G.

● *Human resources issues in education.* Ontario Institute for Studies in Education. University of Toronto.

● *Monograph on quality in post-compulsory education.* Education Directions.

● *Enterprise based education and training: a literature review.* Monash University/ Australian Council for Educational Research.

ISBN 92-64-10030-X
New Challenges for Educational Research
© OECD 2003

PART II

Chapter 5

Education Research and Development in New Zealand
Background report
by New Zealand Ministry of Education
February 2001

Abstract. *This chapter presents the background report prepared by the Ministry of Education, New Zealand for the OECD review of New Zealand's educational R&D system. The report is centered around four main themes :*

1. The national policy and agenda for educational R&D;

2. The organisation and funding of the educational R&D system;

3. The outcomes of educational R&D in terms of teaching and learning, and policy-making; and

4. The strategies for interaction between researchers, practitioners and policy-makers.

5.1. Introduction

The Centre for Educational Research and Innovation (CERI) at the OECD has initiated a set of reviews of national educational research and development systems. The purpose is to review the extent to which the educational research and development system within a country is functioning as an effective means for creating, collating and distributing the knowledge on which practitioners and policy-makers can draw. The aim is broader than a review focused on the quality of the research delivered, rather, the Review Team is interested in the contribution of educational research and development to the knowledge base of education in a learning society.

Educational research and development is broadly defined for the purposes of this Review. The Review Team endorses this definition of educational research and development offered in the 1995 OECD report *Educational research and development – trends, issues and challenges*.

"Educational research and development is a systematic, original investigation or inquiry and associated development activities concerning the social, cultural, economic and political contexts within which educational systems operate and learning takes place; the purposes of education; the processes of teaching, learning and personal development of children, youth and adults; the work of educators; the resources and organisational arrangements to support educational work; the policies and strategies to achieve educational objectives; and the social, cultural, political and economic outcomes of education." (OECD 1995, p. 37)

The Review emphasises that educational research and development is conceived as a multidisciplinary research field and much research and development that is relevant to education will be occurring within other disciplines.

The context

There are several important contextual features within which a review of educational research and development in New Zealand needs to be placed.

Political, economic and social change

In the mid 1980s New Zealand entered a period of dramatic economic and social change. It moved quickly from being a country with a protected economy, to one which demonstrated a commitment to a market model by removing tariffs on imports and subsidies for exporters. In line with the removal of government protection of the economy, there was a move to cutback the size of the government bureaucracy and to reduce the role of central government in social as well as economic affairs.

Along with the reduction in the government bureaucracy emerged a greater emphasis on accountability for government spending, and a move towards contracting – particularly in health and social services. While contracting has not gained as firm a foothold in education as in health and social services, educational research and development is one part of the sector that has been strongly influenced by a shift from institutional funding to contract funding.

Education reforms

As part of the economic and social reforms education administration was decentralised to individual schools through the Education Act of 1989. Each school is now governed by an elected board of trustees, which is responsible for the effective management of the school. The board of trustees – usually comprising 3-7 parent representatives, the principal and a staff representative – is the employer of all staff, responsible for teacher performance, oversees the implementation of the curriculum and manages the school finances and property. All of these were previously the responsibility of the government through the Department of Education. Boards of Trustees are accountable to the Crown, and their performance is monitored by the *Education Review Office (ERO)*.

Schools receive a bulk grant based on pupil numbers to cover running costs. During the 1990s there was a government initiative towards the bulk funding of teachers' salaries as well, however this was resisted in some quarters and has been discontinued by the current Government.

Concurrent with these major changes to schools' organisation and management was the implementation of a new curriculum covering the span of compulsory schooling. *The New Zealand Curriculum Framework: Te Anga Matauranga o Aotearoa* (1993) sets out the overall policy direction for the school curriculum. It includes the principles that underpin the curriculum and describes seven essential learning areas, eight sets of essential skills and the commonly held attitudes and values which should be developed and reinforced through the school-based curriculum. National curriculum statements which detail what students are expected to learn at each age level in each of the essential learning areas have been progressively introduced through the 1990s. The curriculum statements are published in English and in Te Reo Maori for use in Maori-medium education.

Tertiary sector reform

Tertiary sector reform has also been dramatic through the 1990s. The sector has been transformed from one with a small number of academically focused universities, and a number of vocationally focused polytechnics, to one with a much greater number and diversity of institutions, including private training establishments, offering a wide range of academic and vocational courses. The entitlement to award degrees is no longer solely in the hands of the established universities.

One significant development is that all universities, colleges of education, polytechnics or wananga (a tertiary institution that maintains, advances and disseminates knowledge regarding Maori tradition and Maori custom) established under the Education Act 1989 are required to undertake research as well as teaching.

As with early childhood centres, tertiary institutions are bulk funded for running costs and salaries. Government funding has been reduced and student fees have been significantly increased to make up the shortfall. Tertiary institutions are under much more pressure than previously to generate revenue.

Bi-culturalism

Aotearoa-New Zealand is a bi-cultural nation. The document which defines the relation between the Crown (as represented primarily through the New Zealand Government) and the indigenous Maori people is the Treaty of Waitangi. The importance of its bi-cultural heritage has emerged over the last 20 years or so as a critical issue underpinning national activities in New Zealand.

In education this is most obvious through the emergence of kohanga reo – Maori language early childhood centres, and kura kaupapa Maori – primary schools offering education completely in the Maori language, and, more recently, wharekura – a new kura kauapapa Maori secondary option which accommodates students wanting to continue in kura kaupapa Maori beyond the primary school level. Maori language immersion classes and bi-lingual classes can also be found in some schools.

In relation to educational research and development, the appropriateness of education initiatives for Maori children is of prime interest to educators and virtually all research and development projects include some investigation of this dimension. In addition, kaupapa Maori research is a thriving strand of research with its own distinct research methodology.

This paper

This background paper has been prepared for the Review Team prior to its visit to New Zealand. The paper is designed to provide the information

116

specifically requested by the Team, and is organised under the four key themes of the Review. These are:

- the extent to which there is a national policy, and or national agenda for educational research and development;
- how the educational research and development system is organised and funded;
- evidence that educational research and development is contributing to improvements in practice and is informing policy;
- the nature and extent of formal and informal interactions between researchers, policy-makers and practitioners.

This paper was prepared primarily from material gathered in recent interviews with a small number of key informants (listed in Appendix 5.1) identified by the Ministry of Education, and from examination of a range of documents from both government and non-government sources. Documentary sources that discuss educational research and development are scarce however, and their contribution to this report has been secondary to that made by key informants.

5.2. A national policy and agenda for educational research and development

Is there a national policy and agenda for educational research and development?

Informants agree that until very recently there has been nothing resembling a national policy or agenda for educational research and development.

Historically, educational research and development has been fragmented, largely small-scale and often driven by short-term policy agendas, or by the interests of individuals or groups of researchers. There have been some attempts to establish research priorities with the collaboration of the educational research community, policy-makers and practitioners (NZCER 1997), but such initiatives do not appear to have been sustained or reviewed.

More recently however the Minister of Education has indicated that government-funded education research should be more in tune with long-term objectives, and has given the Government's commitment to strengthening the research base that underpins robust, evidence-based policy.*

In line with the Minister's commitment to establishing longer-term objectives for educational research and development, the Ministry of Education

---

* Hon. Trevor Mallard. Press Release 4/10/00.

has recently been involved in a *Strategic Research Initiative* (SRI). The SRI was designed to ensure that current policy work continues to be underpinned by sound research, and that the Ministry of Education's strategic information base enables it to anticipate future policy initiatives.

Two important phases of the SRI have been completed:

- The Ministry commissioned nine "state-of-the-art" literature reviews to provide an understanding of current thinking and developments in a range of key areas. The reviews took a broad look at the literature as well as identifying gaps in knowledge and the nature of research that might address those gaps. Details of the nine reviews can be found in Appendix 5.2.

- A formal consultation with educational researchers, policy-makers and practitioners on priorities for research and the establishment of a research agenda. Held as a stand-alone consultation, there was considerable enthusiasm from informants for further consultation and collaboration on national educational research and development priorities.

The SRI relates solely to Ministry of Education commissioned educational research and development. However, despite a relatively small budget, a high proportion of research is funded by government and this gives the SRI the status of a *de facto* national policy.

With such a recent development no comment can be made about monitoring and evaluation, nor about how effectively it steers educational research and development.

The main themes and topics in educational research and development.

The nine state-of-the-art literature reviews commissioned by the Ministry of Education in 1999 give a good indication of what the Ministry considered to be the main themes within educational research at that time. Full details of the reviews are in Appendix 5.2. The topics covered by the reviews are:

- the effects of family and community resources on education outcomes;

- early childhood education;

- the effects of curriculum and assessment on education outcomes;

- the effects of school governance, ownership, organisation and management on education outcomes;

- the effects of school resourcing on education outcomes;

- post compulsory education;

- human capital development in organisations;

- influence of peer effects on learning outcomes; and

- enterprise based education and training.

NEW CHALLENGES FOR EDUCATIONAL RESEARCH – ISBN 92-64-10030-X – © OECD 2003

Informants for this report were asked about themes in educational research and development over the last 10 years. There was much consistency between the list above and informants' identification of prevailing and emerging themes.

Prevailing themes

The following themes were identified by informants as having been to the forefront of educational research and development over the past decade.

Education reforms: One strand of research that has been well-developed over the past decade has been measuring the impact of the educational reforms. A prime example of this type of research is the *Smithfield Project* (Lauder *et al*. 1994), a longitudinal study of the impact of educational reforms on students' choices and outcomes. There is a view that some of this research has been ideologically driven as a critique of government policy. Another example is NZCER's longitudinal NZCER monitoring the impact of the 1989 education reforms – *The Impact of Education Reforms from 1989*. Between 1989-99, the research project repeatedly surveyed principals, trustees, parents and teachers about the impact of the reforms on primary and intermediate schools.

Assessment: Another theme that has received attention has been assessment practices both at a national and at individual level. This reflects a growing interest in educational outcomes. Some examples include research towards a coherent strategy of national assessment; participation in large scale international studies such as the *Third International Mathematics and Science Study (TIMSS)* and the *Programme for Internal Student Assessment (PISA)*; research into the performance of a sample of children across the country to provide national monitoring of the education systems; and the development of *Assessment Resource Banks (ARBs)* designed as a very practical resource for teachers.

Students at risk: Students at risk of failure and of under-achievement have been the subject of much research. In particular, research and development into how to improve the school achievement of Maori students has been a consistent theme over the past decade. Gender and socio-economic class, as well as ethnicity, have received attention and have moved from being explanatory variables in educational research to being the subject of investigation in their own right in relation to their impact on student achievement.

School improvement: Customised school improvement projects have been initiated in areas of the country where students were considered to be at risk through the poor quality of some of the schools. Some of these projects are being evaluated concurrently, supporting another strand of the research agenda – school improvement.

Indigenous education: Alongside the development of the kura kaupapa Maori model for indigenous education has run a strand of research into indigenous education, which as well as being of great value to New Zealand is considered by several people interviewed for this report to be of international standing.

Emerging themes

Teaching and learning: A theme in the research currently enjoying something of a resurgence of interest is the impact of teaching on learning. While there has since 1992 been a substantial research project investigating the link between teaching and leaning in New Zealand, informants felt that research around issues of teacher quality and the quality of teaching have been somewhat eclipsed in that period but are again gathering momentum in educational research and development.

Literacy and numeracy: Improving both the literacy and numeracy of New Zealand students is currently receiving attention at policy level, and this is being reflected in the research agenda.

How much attention is given in the educational research to trends in the economy and society?

The informants interviewed were confident that educational researchers in this country do take account of trends in economy and society. Examples given include the emphasis placed by the sector on research into student under-achievement and its link with socio-economic status; and the research interest in education management and leadership which has sprung directly from the education reforms of the late 1980s and early 1990s.

That said, there was an agreement that the sector is much stronger on "snapshot", rather than longitudinal research and that this limits the analysis of the impact of trends in economy and society. The view was also expressed that in general education researchers are more open to, and in sympathy with, the interests of social scientists than those of economists, and that there could be a better dialogue between education research and economists.

Initiatives to collect and present information on evidence-based research results for use in practice

There are few concerted initiatives to present research results for use in practice. Two that were mentioned are the long-standing NZCER publication *SET*, designed for practitioners, and the more recent Ministry of Education on-line resource *Te Kete Ipurangi (TKI)*, a bi-lingual portal education website which aims to provide New Zealand school communities with easy access to useful information, including research information, on the Internet.

There are other more project-based examples of research that has presented its findings in such a way as to make them immediately useful to practitioners.

The reports produced by the *National Education Monitoring Project (NEMP)* are considered by informants to be a good example of evidence-based research results presented in a way that makes them immediately available for use by practitioners. Informants agreed however, that there are challenges in presenting research findings to practitioners in a way they see they can use and are prepared to spend time absorbing.

The evaluation running concurrently to the SEMO project is considered to be producing evidence based results that are influencing practice in the area as well as policy.

Initiatives to collect and present information on evidence-based research results for use in policy-making

The SRI is a concerted attempt to enhance the links between policy and research by ensuring that the research commissioned is of direct relevance to policy, and that in turn policy development can be informed by quality research.

Informants had specific examples of research results that directly informed policy prior to the SRI. These include:

- The *Third International Mathematics and Science Study* (TIMSS) which indicated that at some levels the achievement of New Zealand's students in mathematics was below that of students in comparable countries. The TIMSS led to the establishment of the Maths and Science Taskforce, and from there to policy initiatives within the primary school sector.

- The evaluation reports of the SEMO work in South Auckland is considered to be a good example of a research project directly informing policy and implementation and thereby influencing practice.

- The findings of the NEMP directly inform policy development. An example given is the Literacy Taskforce established by the Government following some of the findings of the NEMP which indicated areas of underachievement in New Zealand students' literacy. The Literacy Taskforce in turn established the Literacy Experts Group charged, amongst other responsibilities, with summarising research results to inform policy development.

- The *Competent Children* study has been and is a significant resource – this longitudinal study looks at what effects early childhood care and education contexts have for children. It has tracked a cohort of children since before they turned 5 years of age – the current phase of the study is investigating the sample of children at age 12. The study is the only one of its kind in the New Zealand context and has, over an extended period, influenced policy and practice.

Is educational research and development evaluated?

The SRI has been peer reviewed nationally and internationally in a way that has exposed the research agenda of the major funder of educational research and development to international scrutiny. The state-of-art literature reviews underpinning the initiative have also been peer reviewed.

Currently the Ministry of Education and the *New Zealand Association for Research in Education (NZARE)* have jointly commissioned a project to map the educational research and development capacity and capability throughout New Zealand. Although largely descriptive, the project has an evaluative component. The findings are to be delivered shortly.

At a project level educational research is evaluated. Academic research is exposed to peer review, especially at the point of publication. Research commissioned by the Ministry of Education is increasingly subject to peer review by experts either within New Zealand or in other countries. Development projects are less likely to have formal external review, although are likely to be the subject of evaluation.

At an institutional level, research centres may be evaluated, for example an internal university review of a faculty or department, but the indicators would not normally include the quality of the research produced. NZCER research is peer-reviewed.

Does the national policy encourage the internationalisation of the research endeavour?

Informants were of the view that while educational researchers in this country recognise the importance of the internationalisation of education research and seek to play an active part in it, their motivation is largely individual and not as a result of being encouraged to do so by a national policy.

Educational researchers tend to have particularly good links at a regional level in Australia and the Pacific. Beyond this region the points of reference for education tend to be the United Kingdom, Canada and to a lesser extent the United States. Giving papers at or attending conferences is the main way of participating in the international research community.

As well as the set of state-of-the-art literature reviews, the Ministry of Education on occasion commissions international literature reviews to inform research or policy initiatives.

Some universities are seeking to be part of international coalitions of institutions to enhance and internationalise their research and teaching efforts. For example, both Auckland University and AUT are part of international tertiary education groups.

Indigenous education is one area in which some informants consider that New Zealand has a high level of expertise and could be making a more substantial contribution internationally. They felt more could be done to encourage New Zealand researchers and policy-makers in this area to participate internationally.

5.3. Organisation and funding of educational research and development systems

The educational research and development sector in New Zealand was described by several informants as "fragmented" or "piecemeal" meaning that the sector has lacked coherence and, until recently, any form of national policy or agenda. Research expertise is concentrated in a few pockets of excellence, generally in the larger universities, and NZCER. Centralised contestable funding has created an environment where much of the research effort is determined by the policy agenda, and funding for longer term research can be hard to find.

Centres of educational research and development

Educational research expertise is largely concentrated in the established universities, and in the *New Zealand Council for Educational Research (NZCER)*, with the new universities, polytechnics and the colleges of education beginning to build a research capacity. Development work is more evenly spread, with the colleges of education often taking a leading role.

As well as research undertaken by academics within departments or schools of education, some of the larger universities also have centres or institutes with a particular research focus. Examples include: in Auckland, *IRI – the International Research Institute for Maori and Indigenous Education* and the *Woolf Fisher Centre*; in Waikato, the *Institute for Research in Learning and Teaching* and the *Centre for Science, Mathematics and Technology Education Research*; the *Educational Research and Development Centre* at Massey University; and the *Educational Assessment Research Unit* and the *Children's Issues Centre* at Otago University.

Research in universities is funded from income generated by student numbers, research contracts and, if applications are successful, grant funding. Universities also have access to graduate students which enhances their research capacity.

With the possible exception of the University of Auckland, in international terms the institutes and departments of education are small, and informants felt that research expertise is in many cases still based around the interests and efforts of individuals rather than being institutionalised.

NZCER is a recognised centre of expertise in educational research, although in recent times considered by some informants to have been somewhat eclipsed by the larger universities. NZCER is an independent statutory body which aims to foster educational research of a high standard and to disseminate its results. NZCER's main funding sources include a purchase agreement with the Government, income from research contracts, and revenue from sales. (NZCER 2000)

The Ministry of Education has its own research expertise, however much of the capacity of the Ministry's Research Division is directed towards contributing to international assessment projects and to the establishment and management of research and evaluation projects. Other divisions of the Ministry also undertake research but if it is of any scale this is likely to be contracted out and managed by the Research Division.

Substantive programmes of educational research and development

A range of substantive educational research and development programmes were mentioned by the people interviewed for this report. They include research directed towards better assessment of educational outcomes such as:

- The NEMP – based at Otago University the project aims to get a broad picture of the achievements and other educational outcomes of a representative sample of students in New Zealand at school years 4 and 8.

- ARBs – this NZCER managed project is developing assessment resources for mathematics, science, and English from levels 3 to 6 of the curriculum. ARB items are designed to assist schools to monitor student performance against typical performance of student's nationally.

- The Development of Literacy and Numeracy Instruments for students in Year 5 and Year 7 in English and Maori – this is a joint project between the University of Auckland and the Education Testing Centre of the University of New South Wales. The project involves the development of literacy and numeracy tools that teachers will be able to use with students to assess their skills and knowledge in relation to the New Zealand English and mathematics curricula, and for students learning in Maori-medium settings, their skills and knowledge in Te Reo Maori and pangarau.

Another substantive programme is the evaluation of this school improvement project:

- Evaluation of initiatives to strengthen education in Otara and Mangere SEMO – this evaluation consists of four studies designed to cover how the initiatives and their implementation have unfolded, and the extent to which initiatives have improved the quality of relationships in the interests of better education and increased the capacity of schools and the community to sustain progress.

Four other large scale research projects, the last two of which are largely complete are:

- An integrated research programme established by the Ministry of Education and designed to inform and evaluate the development and implementation of *Special Education 2000*, a new policy for learners with special needs which began in 1997. The research programme includes: database validation exercises; a series of literature reviews on resourcing, effective practice and provision; evaluations of specific programmes; and a longitudinal evaluation of the policy.

- *Competent Children* – this NZCER longitudinal study looks at what effects early childhood care and education contexts have for children's learning and development.

- *Understanding Teaching and Learning (ULT)* – a University of Canterbury Department of Education longitudinal project, ULT first developed a descriptive model of classroom learning processes and has subsequently analysed the effects of gender and ethnicity on children's learning and is moving to identify the impact of teachers and curriculum on pupil learning.

- *Educational Performance and Opportunities (The Smithfield Project)* – This longitudinal study examines the impact of education reforms on primary and secondary students' choices and outcomes. (Ministry of Education 1998, 1999a, 2000b.)

The funding of educational research and development

The funding of educational research and development in New Zealand is highly centralised, with the Ministry of Education being the primary funder. Some education research and development is also funded through the Research, Science and Technology Vote, however with that funding stream there is no strand dedicated to educational research and development. Funding strands available under Research, Science and Technology include the *Foundation for Research, Science and Technology (FRST)*, the *Health Research Council (HRC)*, the *Public Good Science Fund (PSGF)* and the *Royal Society of New Zealand* administered *Marsden Fund* for university-based research. The researchers interviewed for this report indicated that in reality it is extremely difficult for researchers in education to access funds from any of these sources.

University departments, polytechnics and colleges of education draw some research funding from student tuition fees *(EFTS)*. Some university departments have also been successful in achieving funding from overseas foundations for specific research projects, however attracting offshore funding is uncommon. Some researchers have also had success in obtaining small amounts of funding for projects from other government agencies such

Figure 5.1. **Funding for Educational R&D delivered through Vote Education (New Zealand Ministry of Education)**

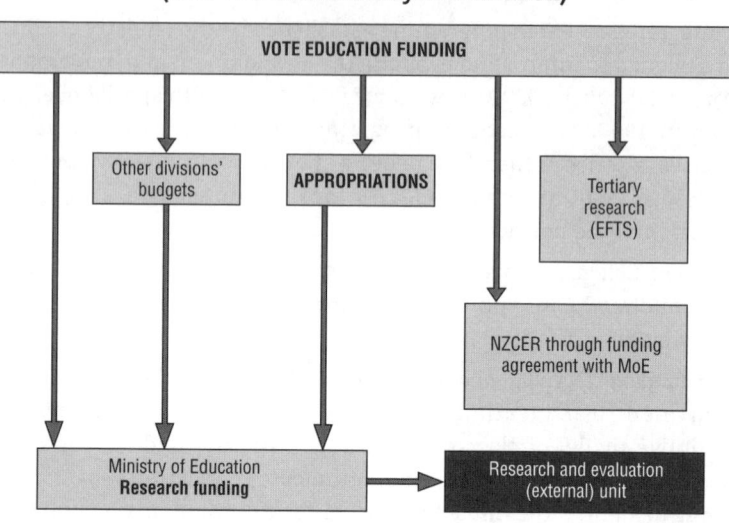

as the Ministry of Social Policy, Ministry of Justice and the Department of Labour.

Figure 5.1 shows how Vote Education funding for educational research and development is delivered through EFTS funding, the New Zealand Council for Educational Research and the Ministry of Education.

The Ministry has an internal research capacity (*i.e.* personnel who undertake research) and also contracts research to external providers. Commissioned research and development projects are funded by appropriations attached to specific policy initiatives and the budgets of Ministry Divisions. The Ministry's Research Division also has a small budget for commissioning projects with a strategic policy focus. The Ministry's SRI is the process being used to develop a set of research priorities to determine how to best use this resource.

Table 5.1 provides a summary of funding distributed to the educational research community from 1 July 1997 (start of 1997/8 financial year) to 30 June 2001 (end of 2000/1 financial year) through the Ministry of Education's Research Division. This summary includes all educational R&D activities funded in that five-year period.

The Ministry of Education is also responsible for negotiating annually a purchase agreement with NZCER.

The project-based nature of research funding, and the operational focus of the primary funder are seen by some as having significant implications for the type of educational research and development undertaken in New Zealand, as well as for workforce development.

Table 5.1.   **Ministry of Education expenditure on educational R&D
1 July 1997-30 June 2001 (through Research Division)**

Source of funding	NZD
Budget appropriations	16 500 000
Budget appropriations for specific programmes and or policies	(2 300 000)
Assessment pool – reviews, R&D and evaluations	(3 200 000)
Assessment Resource Banks	(4 000 000)
National Education Monitoring Project	(7 000 000)
Funding from Research Division Operations	3 600 000
Funding from other Division Operations	1 200 000
Other (includes external funds and inter-agency)	200 000
Total	**21 500 000**

Note: Costs of individual projects are listed in the Research Division's Annual Research Reports. As projects span financial years, figures have been rounded to the nearest NZD 100 000.

Research over time, and research into areas that are not seen as having current operational relevance find it hard to attract funding. One area that is currently attracting the interest of policy-makers is the contribution of teaching to learning outcomes. However, longitudinal studies into the relationship between teaching and learning which have produced results of great value, have in years past struggled for funding as the policy priorities and research effort have been directed elsewhere.

The difficulty of building the capacity of the educational research and development workforce is seen as in large part related to project-based funding that does not support the development and maintenance of centres of research expertise which can train and supervise new researchers.

In the view of some informants the fact that the Ministry of Education funds the most significant proportion of educational R&D aside from EFTS funding and the small size of the research community make it easier for more established researchers to attract funding than for their less experienced colleagues.

The educational research and development workforce characteristics

A research project mapping the capacity and capability of the educational research workforce is soon to present its findings and should be available when the Review Team visits.

The educational research and development community in New Zealand is small. Researchers are based in tertiary institutions or allied institutes, NZCER, the Ministry of Education, or work independently as contractors providing research services. The workforce profile is characterised by some established, experienced researchers, either working in comparative isolation, or as part of larger teams for specific projects. The people interviewed for this report were concerned that the sector is not currently building sufficient capacity for the future by developing the skills of younger researchers. The reasons for this are two-fold, a lack of educational research centres with enough of a critical mass to enable such development to take place; and an approach to contracting and funding research that does not support the infrastructural costs such development would require.

There is a range of discipline backgrounds amongst educational researchers. Historically research was dominated by educational psychologists but, partly as a result of the requirement in the 1989 Education Act for all tertiary institutes to be undertaking research, the workforce is now more diverse.

One informant expressed the view that there seems to be a weakening of some of the traditional disciplines such as education history, philosophy and sociology, in favour of new emphases including post-modernism, feminism, kaupapa Maori research and practitioner effectiveness.

Informants interviewed for this report noted some gaps in expertise. They identified a need for more Maori researchers and other researchers who can work effectively with Maori, and a need for more researchers with well developed quantitative analytical skills.

Collaboration between disciplines is increasing at a project level, however, in the view of some people interviewed for this report, seldom is it systemic or embedded in the infrastructure.

5.4. The impact of educational research and development on practice and its input to policy-making: evidence that educational research and development is improving the quality of teaching and learning, of educational institutions, or of the management of education

Teaching and learning

Informants for the report were divided as to whether there was evidence that educational research and development is improving the quality of teaching and learning. Most agreed that there was some evidence that research was improving practice but that the evidence was not extensive.

New National Curriculum Statements have been progressively replacing old syllabuses since 1992. The Ministry of Education is currently undertaking a curriculum stock take which will provide more information about how changes in the curriculum over have been put into action and ways of improving its implementation. One element of the stock take is a *National School Sampling Study* that will seek feedback from teachers about the effectiveness of the curriculum in practice.

Informants commented that the longitudinal research necessary to demonstrate the impact of an initiative on teaching and learning is uncommon in New Zealand. The new curricula that have been introduced over the last 10 years are a good example of a major initiative with an enormous potential impact on teaching and learning, yet no systematic, large-scale evaluation has accompanied their implementation.

Evaluations of individual projects have been commissioned for some time. Only more recently has it become more common for evaluations to be initiated at the time programmes are implemented in a way that allows systematic evidence to be gathered about whether research-based initiatives are improving outcomes.

Informants cited some examples of evidence. They include:

- the evaluation of the SEMO initiative in South Auckland which has intensive collaboration between researchers and practitioners and from which there is clear evidence that the findings of the evaluation are influencing practice;

- piloting of programmes for literacy gain which are strongly research based are showing promising results;

- an evaluation of the *Books in Homes* project which provides children in schools in the lowest socio-economic areas with books of their own to take home. The literacy skills of students are assessed when they join the programme and then again one year later;

- the research-based development work undertaken by IRI – *The International Research Institute for Maori and Indigenous Education* has been shown to be influencing practice in kura kaupapa Maori;

- the ARBs are influencing assessment practices in schools;

- later phases of the NEMP have demonstrated that deficits identified in earlier phases have been addressed in the classroom;

- developments in the early childhood sector, particularly the new curriculum *Te Whariki* and the emphasis on professional development are clearly related to research which began in the 1980s.

Educational institutions

Other than SEMO, a school improvement/research partnership, informants were hard pressed to think of specific examples of evidence that research had improved the quality of educational institutions. However, some commented that there is now much more emphasis on the environment within which education is provided, and a recognition of the need to provide appropriate environments – such as kura kaupapa Maori.

The management of education

The management of education has received considerable attention in the research following the significant changes introduced by the 1989 reforms. Whether the research has contributed to improving the quality of management, or simply documented the changes, is less clear.

Research into the governance, organisation and management of education is a good example of research following a major shift in policy and practice rather than informing it – something several informants consider to be a characteristic of educational research in New Zealand.

One example of research into management, which is also an example of research following a policy decision, is a project commissioned by the Ministry of Education into school "clusters". A cluster in this context is where small self-managing schools, often with very limited management capacity, form a local grouping for some administrative purposes thus reducing the workload for each school. The research showed that clustering did reduce the administrative workload for each principal, but not the overall workload.

Evidence that educational research and development is contributing to policy-making

Informants considered that there is evidence that educational research and development is contributing to policy-making at a national level. This is in part because the Ministry of Education, with its policy focus, is frequently the funder and has had a major influence on setting the educational research agenda.

Recently, through the SRI the Ministry of Education has demonstrated a keener interest in a wider range of research activity than had previously been shown. The SRI has also signalled a commitment to ensuring that research will more directly inform policy, and that policy-makers can play an active part in determining research questions.

Researchers acknowledge that the link between research and policy cannot always be a direct one. Research findings are seldom unequivocal, and often raise as many questions as they answer. The researchers interviewed for this report, however, consider that education policy-makers take an active interest in research, and that frequent citation of the evidence base when preparing policy papers is a demonstration of their willingness to use research findings.

The Taskforces and subsequent initiatives in literacy and numeracy were cited as evidence that policy in those areas has been responsive to research findings.

Policy changes within the early childhood sector, particularly in the area of qualifications are another example of educational research making a direct contribution to policy development.

Evaluation of the contribution of educational research and development to practice and to policy-making

There are no ongoing or systematic initiatives that evaluate the contribution of educational research and development to either practice or to policy-making.

A culture of evaluation is now becoming more established in New Zealand, Until recently, despite evaluations of individual projects there has been, in the view of informants, a lack of systematic and substantive evaluation programmes or meta-evaluations that can provide good information on the sector's contribution to practice or to policy.

There are isolated examples of overview and commentary on the contribution of educational research and development at papers presented at NZARE and NZCER conferences.

5.5. Interaction between producers of research, practitioners and policy-makers

The relationships between researchers, practitioners and policy-makers

Informants interviewed for this report spoke positively of relationships between researchers, practitioners and policy-makers. The small size of the education research and development community supports strong relationships. It is clear however that these relationships are largely informal, often project related, and with practitioners in particular, most well developed at a local level. Relationships are supported by a history of practitioners moving into policy and of researchers being welcome in schools.

Established researchers are known to one another, and are aware of work in progress throughout the country. Researchers also know the key policy-makers in their fields, and several indicated they feel quite free to initiate discussion with those policy-makers and feel confident their opinions will be taken seriously.

Having national education policies and programmes and a relatively homogenous compulsory schooling sector means that funds permitting, research projects can be on a national scale. It also means that research undertaken anywhere in the country is likely to have relevance throughout the nation. This creates a high level of interest in research findings researchers, policy-makers and some practitioners.

Few formal channels of communication exist between the three groups. The NZARE conferences were mentioned as an opportunity for communication between researchers and policy-makers, but few practitioners attend. The forum to discuss the draft statement of SRI research priorities was highly regarded as an opportunity for dialogue between stakeholders and the hope was expressed that it will be repeated.

How the findings of educational research and development activities are disseminated to practitioners and policy-makers

Dissemination to practitioners

Disseminating research findings to practitioners in a way that is meaningful to them and useful to their practice is regarded as one of the greatest challenges facing the educational research and development sector.

Educational research findings and development findings are currently disseminated to practitioners (and others) in a range of ways including through:

- academic journals such as the New Zealand Journal of Education Studies;
- weekly general circulation newspapers such as *The New Zealand Education Review;*
- SET, a publication produced by NZCER three times a year for schools contains summaries of research relevant to teachers;
- brief summaries of current and completed research produced by the Research Division for the Ministry of Education's *Annual Research Report;*
- *Te Kete Ipurangi (TKI)* the Ministry of Education's website for teachers;
- summaries of research produced by the teacher unions the *New Zealand Educational Institute (NZEI)* and the *Post-primary Teachers Association (PPTA)* and distributed to members;
- seminars on research and topics of current interest, for example *National Assessment Regional Seminars* jointly organised by the Ministry of Education, NZEI, and the University of Canterbury were held in 2000;
- researchers often give presentation to professional organisations and educators' conferences and seminars;
- research reports, and associated bulletins, targeted directly to practitioners such as those produced by NEMP and sent, free of charge, to all schools;
- over the Internet, schools can register their interest in the resources produced by the ARBs project and download these free of charge;
- "Input" – the NZARE newsletter contains summaries of current and recently completed research;
- a wide range of research-based publications are produced by NZCER and available for purchase, these are promoted in schools through a regular newsletter and targeted promotions;

- summaries of research findings are often given to participants in research;
- a range summary reports produced by the ERO, drawn from observations made by Education Review Officers during school reviews.

There was agreement among those interviewed that disseminating research findings in written form has limited appeal to practitioners. Approximately two-thirds of schools have a subscription to the highly regarded SET publication, however it is not known how widely read it is once it is in the school. Many of the other publications available from NZCER are also purchased by between a third and two-thirds of schools.

Informants agreed that there needs to be more work done on translating research findings from "researcher-speak" and "policy-speak" to "practitioner-speak".

Informants were unsure who the key "mediators" of research findings are, beyond those who produce the resources listed above. Some were of the view that the small size and relative informality of the educational research and development community allows researchers, practitioners and policy-makers to communicate directly without the need for mediation.

There was no clear view about the role of the professional development community in mediating research results, but it needs to be acknowledged that none of the informants interviewed is primarily involved in teacher professional development. Some informants commented that prior to the education reforms, school inspectors would often fulfil this role, linking teachers to research and development that was relevant to their practice. A recent review of the ERO proposed a closer alignment of assessment and improvement functions, and that the advisory functions of the Office be enhanced. (State Services Commission 2000). Another view holds that Colleges of Education play a part in mediating research results – advisors in schools work base their practice on recent research, and advanced qualification courses run by colleges include applied research components.

Policy-makers

Reports of all research commissioned by the Ministry of Education Research Division are made available to the Division as a contract requirement. This ensures they can be made available to relevant policy-makers within the Ministry. Research and development projects of any size are overseen by an advisory committee which will include key policy-makers who will therefore be familiar with the progress and development of a project as well as having access to the final report.

When major research findings are available the Ministry of Education develops a communications strategy that will include will include press releases and summaries of the research made available to education journalists. Research reports completed for the Research Division are published by the Ministry and are available on request.

How receptive are teachers, school managers and policy-makers to research results?

Teachers

Informants interviewed for this report regard New Zealand teachers as innovative and willing to try new things. However, they are perceived as being largely interested in developments with an immediate application to their own practice. The most obvious reason for this focus on utility is their heavy workload, but also perhaps a lack of weight given to research in pre-service and in-service teacher training. With an increased focus on research within colleges of education this may change, and that teachers may become more confident in their ability to absorb and use research findings.

Informants recognised the need to involve teachers more in setting the agenda for research, and to create more opportunities for them to participate in projects in order to maximise their ownership of the findings.

School managers

In New Zealand school managers are principals, and over half of them are teaching principals which means they carry a teaching load as well as taking responsibility for the management of the school. With devolution central to the education reforms, the management and administrative responsibilities of principals have increased substantially. It is inevitable that this will have required principals to reprioritise their workload and it may be that keeping abreast of current educational research and development has a lower priority amongst their responsibilities than was the case prior to the reforms. Even so, principals use invited researchers to speak to them, and increasing numbers are undertaking Masters of Education, and as a result, using more research, understanding what is available and what is good quality research.

The culture established in the school by the principal is seen as being crucial to whether teachers are aware of and receptive to research findings. Teachers need to be encouraged to see research as relevant and to incorporate findings of research in their practice.

Policy-makers

As discussed elsewhere in this report policy-makers are seen as receptive to educational research, although this is to be expected when the policy agenda has a major influence on the research and development commissioned, or when researchers themselves initiate research that influences national policy.

Does the educational research and development community draw from and contribute to the international debate?

Most informants consider New Zealand's educational researchers and developers to be active participants in the international educational debates. New Zealand is a committed participant in OECD and UNESCO initiatives, and an active member of the *International Association for the Evaluation of Educational Achievement (IEA)*.

A dissenting view was strongly expressed by one informant who considers the educational research community in New Zealand to be insular, and not making the contribution internationally that it should be, given the calibre of the work taking place here.

Specifically, informants considered that New Zealand is making and could possibly make further contributions internationally in the areas of early childhood education, indigenous education, teaching and learning, literacy, assessment and monitoring, and education organisation and management.

5.6. Knowledge management in the learning society

This background report is asked to reflect on whether this country is moving towards Mode 2 knowledge production in education, and to identify initiatives which may increase its capacity for successful production, mediation and application of knowledge.

Mode 2 knowledge production as defined by Gibbons *et al.* (1994) as knowledge production which can be described as:

- applied;
- problem-focused;
- trans-disciplinary;
- demand-driven;
- entrepreneurial;
- accountability tested; and
- embedded in networks.

The report is asked to report New Zealand's progress by identifying initiatives under eight themes.

Developing a commitment to knowledge management.

In terms of the management of knowledge within educational research and development, the SRI is one attempt to bring some coherence and direction, and the widespread awareness of this initiative may enable it to act as a focus for knowledge management.

The requirement in the 1989 Education Act that all tertiary institutions undertake research has given knowledge production a new profile in colleges of education. Raising the awareness and increasing the research skills of practitioners in pre-service training may support them to see their professional knowledge as a resource that can and should be shared.

One example of a more global commitment to the management of knowledge gained through research and development is the Foresight Project. The Foresight Project began in 1998 and was scheduled to enable revised priorities for publicly funded research, science and technology to be implemented mid 2000. The Foresight Project was not a strategic planning exercise, but rather, an attempt to provide a conceptual framework for plotting paths to a desirable future and for identifying the core competencies needed to create such paths. By developing a focus on foresight the desire was to build an ability to adapt strategically to events and trends as they unfolded.

The Foresight Project had two broad goals:

- Encourage an ongoing process of strategic thinking across diverse communities, as a basis for developing a coherent and forward-looking view of needs and opportunities for new knowledge and technological change.

- Using the insights gained, develop a new set of priorities for the Government's investment in research, science and technology, to take effect in July 2000, in order to complement the diverse strategic intents of other investors. (Ministry of Research, Science and Technology 1998)

The Foresight Project led directly to the Government establishing four high level goals for research, science and technology June 2000. Of these, one is the "innovation goal". This goal is described thus:

Investments under this goal help the overall innovation system to run as effectively as possible. It includes the costs of developing and running the system, ensuring the flow of new ideas through basic research and initiatives to promote the results of research and innovation. (Minister of Research, Science and Technology 2000)

Expanding the role of practitioners in knowledge management

SEMO is one example of a high profile project in which teachers and researchers are collaborating to improve the quality of schools across a region. The partnership has stimulated the active participation of practitioners in schools, and has demonstrated the value of sharing knowledge and experience across schools.

The requirement for all tertiary institutions including colleges of education to undertake research is a clear message to the profession that parishioners must engage with, if not engage in, research.

136

Establishing and using networks for knowledge management

Anecdotal information suggests that rapid developments in the use of information technology in schools, and the increased use of the Internet as an easily accessible source of information and resources is reducing the insularity of some schools.

At a more local level, schools are encouraged to "cluster" to take advantage of professional development opportunities and other forms of support.

However, information from informants suggests that teaching is becoming less of a collective and outward looking endeavour than in the past, and that schools have tended to focus energy inwards in response to the demands of boards of trustees.

Using ICT to support knowledge management

In 1998 the Government launched *Interactive education: an information and communication technologies (ICT) strategy for schools*. This three year strategy costing NZD 16.2 million had two parts: building infrastructure and increasing school capability that welded together existing and new initiatives. (Ministry of Education 1999*b*)

The *Assessment Resource Banks (ARBs)* are collections of assessment resources located on the Internet. They have been developed to help schools and teachers assess students' achievement in mathematics, science and English. Exemplars – available on-line – are also being developed to support literacy programmes by providing teachers with examples of what students might be expected to achieve at each level of the curriculum.

Te Kete Ipurangi (TKI), the Ministry of Education's on-line resource for teachers, is an example of another use of ICT to support knowledge management (*www.tki.org.nz*).

Forging new roles and relationships between researchers and practitioners to better support educational research and development

New science and technology fellowships to allow teachers to spend time working in research institutions and in industry: a first round of applications in 1999/2000 resulted in 35 applicants meeting the required quality standard. A further 30 fellowships were made available later the same year. (Ministry of Education 1999a)

SEMO, discussed elsewhere in this report, is a good example of an initiative that has forged new relationships between researchers and practitioners.

Devising new forms of professional development that reflect and support knowledge management priorities

One result of the education reforms requiring greater accountability to the parent community is that schools perceive that parents are not willing to have teachers out of the classroom for extended periods (more than 1 or 2 days) of professional development. This has led to the abandonment of some successful past initiatives such as drawing together "seed" teachers for professional development. These able and enthusiastic teachers undertook week-long professional development as a group, and then returned to their schools to inspire other teachers.

With the progressive introduction of new curricula, much of the recent professional development has had a curriculum focus, and been delivered through Ministry of Education contracts with colleges of education and other providers.

The professional development aspect of the ICT strategy (see 5.4) is one example of professional development focused on knowledge management.

Integrating knowledge capital and social capital

One of the thrusts of the education reforms was to promote a greater degree of community "ownership" of education. The intention was to make schools more responsive to their communities, and to provide a structure for community input into schools. Research suggests that most schools are able to attract a sufficient number of parent trustees, but that the profile of those trustees reflects the communities from which they are drawn, and that lower decile schools are more likely to have Maori trustees, and trustees without qualifications, than are higher decile schools. (Wylie 1999)

Designing an infrastructure to support knowledge management

Knowledge management in the learning society describes the elements of the infrastructure to support knowledge management. (OECD 2000)

New Zealand has made more progress towards some of these elements than others have. Evidence of progress can be seen in:

- ICT networks linking educational organisations to one another and to other knowledge management resources;
- establishing forums to provide strategies and guidance for education research and development and research foresight exercises;
- developing partnerships between schools and educational researchers.

Less well developed are models of professional development to support knowledge management amongst educational leaders and managers, and establishing and using networks for knowledge management. However, some forms of advanced professional training (*e.g.*, diploma courses in educational management) tend to have a significant research orientation.

5.7. What could be done better in the existing educational research and development system

This report is also asked to comment on what could be done better in the existing research and development system. The key informants interviewed for this report identified several improvements that could be made. These have been grouped under the four themes of this Review.

National policies and agenda for educational research and development

● fostering other funding sources in order to pursue research that may not have current priority on the policy agenda;

● more debate between stakeholders – including government, schools, researchers and communities – to develop a shared view of the current concerns in education;

● more active participation by educational researchers and those involved in educational development projects from New Zealand in international education debates.

Organisation and funding of educational research and development

● more diverse funding sources;

● more active pursuit of overseas funding and international collaboration;

● funding that support the development of a research and development infrastructure;

● funding that encourages more longitudinal studies and more replication of research;

● further analysis of the rich data sets collected by the Ministry of Education.

The outcomes of educational research and development

● more systematic evaluation of research-based development projects;

● more meta-evaluation to establish progress towards goals and to give feedback on the performance of the educational research and development sector.

Strategies for producer-user interaction

● greater engagement of researchers and with practitioners;

● more creative dissemination of research findings and research-based developments;

● greater collaboration between research institutions and amongst disciplines within institutions;

● raising the profile of research in teacher pre-service and in-service training;

● more formalised opportunities for contact between researchers, policy-makers and practitioners.

Bibliography

Gibbons M., C. Limoges, H. Nowotny, S. Schwartzman, P. Scott, and M. Trow, (1994), *The new production of knowledge*. Sage. Cited in, *Reviews of national educational research and development systems*. OECD, March 2000.

Lauder H., D. Hughes, S. Waslander , M. Thrupp, J. McGlinn, S. Newtown, and A. Dupuis (1994), The creation of market competition for education in New Zealand: and empirical analysis of a New Zealand secondary school market, 1990-1993. The Smithfield Project: Phase One. Victoria University of Wellington, Wellington.

Minister of Research, Science and Technology (2000), Transforming New Zealand: challenges and opportunities in research, science and technology.

Ministry of Education (1998), Annual research report 1998-1999, Research Division. Ministry of Education.

Ministry of Education (1999a), Annual research report 1998-1999, Research Division. Ministry of Education.

Ministry of Education. (1999b), Briefing for the incoming Minister of Education.

Ministry of Education. (2000a), Draft statement of strategic research priorities: directions and opportunities.

Ministry of Education (2000b), Annual research report 1999-2000, Research Division. Ministry of Education.

Ministry of Research, Science and Technology (1998), *The Foresight Project*.

New Zealand Council for Educational Research (1997), Priorities for Educational Research in New Zealand: Conference Proceedings. NZCER. Wellington.

New Zealand Government. *Education Act 1989*. Reprinted 1995 with amendments incorporated.

NZCER (2000), Annual Report 1999-2000.

OECD (2000), *Knowledge management in the learning society*. OECD, Paris.

OECD (1995), *Educational research and development: trends, issues and challenges*. OECD, Paris.

Rogers S *et al.* (2000), Report to the Minister of Education: A review of the roles and responsibilities of the Education Review Office. State Services Commission

Wylie C. (1999), *Ten years on: how schools view educational reform*, New Zealand Council for Educational Research, Wellington.

APPENDIX 5.1

Interviewed Persons

Sandie Aiken	Executive Officer Curriculum New Zealand Educational Institute
Robyn Baker	Director New Zealand Council of Educational Research
Jacky Burgon	Research Division Ministry of Education
Brian Findsen	Associate Head School of Education and Social Science
AUT	Alison Gilmore University of Canterbury
John Hattie	Professor Department of Education University of Auckland
John Langley	Director Teacher Registration Board
Rob McIntosh	Group Manager Ministry of Education
Stuart McNaughton	Director Woolf Fisher Research Centre
Roger Peddie	Associate Professor Department of Education University of Auckland
Melissa Weenink	Research Division Ministry of Education

Lynne Whitney   Senior Manager
                                       Research Division
                                       Ministry of Education

Cathy Wylie   Chief Researcher
                                       New Zealand Council of Educational
                                       Research

Appendix 5.2

"State-of-the-Art" Literature Reviews

The Impact of Family and Community Resources on Student Outcomes: An Assessment of the International Literature with Implications for New Zealand, **Stanford University**: Thomas Nechyba; Patrick McEwan; and Diana Older-Aguilar.

Early Childhood Education Literature Review, **Children's Issues Centre – Otago University**: Anne Smith, Grace Grima, Michael Gaffney, Kim Powell, with input from Len Masse and Steve Barnett.

The Effects of Curriculum and Assessment on Pedagogical Approaches and on Education Outcomes, **University of Waikato**: Malcolm Carr; Clive McGee; Alister Jones; Elizabeth McKinley; Beverly Bell; Hugh Barr; and Tina Simpson.

Influence of Peer Effects on Learning Outcomes: A Review of the Literature, **University of Auckland**: Ian Wilkinson; John Hattie; Judith Parr; Michael Townsend; Martin Thrupp; Hugh Lauder; and Tony Robinson.

Literature Review of the Effect of School Resourcing on Education Outcomes, **BERL/Infometrics**: Peter Norton; Kel Sanderson; Tony Booth; and Adolf Stroombergen.

The Effects of School Governance, Ownership, Organisation and Management on Educational Outcomes, John Rentoul and John Rosanowski, with Neil Dempster, Darrell Fisher, Neville Hosking, Roger Hunter, Geoff Pugh, and Geoffrey Walford.

Human Resources Issues in Education, **Ontario Institute for Studies in Education of the University of Toronto**: Michael Fullan and Blair Mascall.

Monograph on Quality in Post-compulsory Education, **Education Directions**: Jeremy Baker; Dave Guerin; and David Woodhouse.

Enterprise-based Education and Training – A Literature Review, **Monash University/Australian Council for Educational Research**: Michael Long; Rose Ryan; Gerald Burke, and Sonnie Hopkins.

Glossary of Acronyms

ARBs	Assessment Resource Banks
BEI	British Education Index
BERA	British Educational Research Association
BPRS	Best Practice Research Scholarships
CERUK	Current Educational Research in United Kingdom
CPRE	Consortium for Policy Research in Education
CREST	Center for Research Educational Standards and Testing
CUREE	Centre for the Use of Research and Evidence in Education
DfEE	Department for Education and Employment
DfES	Department for Education and Skills
DIPF	German Institute for International Education Research
EFTS	Equivalent full-time student (as in EFTS funding)
EPPI Centre	Evidence for Policy and Practice Information and Co-ordinating Centre
ERO	Education Review Office
ESRC	Economic and Social Research Council
FRST	Foundation for Research Science and Technology
GTC	General Teaching Council
HEFCE	Higher Education Funding Council for England
HEI	Higher Education Institute
HRC	Health Research Council
IRI	the International Research Institute for Maori and Indigenous Education
LEA	Local Education Authority
LRDC	Learning Research and Development Centre
NEMP	National Education Monitoring Project
NERF	National Educational Research Forum
NFER	National Foundation for Educational Research
NRC	National Research Council
NUT	National Union of Teachers
NZARE	New Zealand Association of Researchers in Education
NZCER	New Zealand Council for Educational Research
NZEI	New Zealand Educational Institute

Ofsted	Office for Standards in Education
PERINE	Pedagogical and Educational Research Information Network for Europe
PISA	Programme for Internal Student Assessment
PPTA	Post Primary Teachers Association
PSGF	Public Good Science Fund
QCA	The Qualifications and Curriculum Authority
R&D	Research and development
RAE	Research assessment exercise
RSNZ	Royal Society of New Zealand
SEMO	Initiatives to Strengthen Education in Mangere and Otara
SRI	Strategic Research Initiative
TEAC	Tertiary Education Advisory Commission
TIMSS	Third International Mathematics and Science Study
TKI	Te Kete Ipurangi
TTA	Teacher Training Agency
UCET	Universities' Council for the Education of Teachers
WCER	Wisconsin Center for Education Research
WWC	What Works Clearinghouse

NEW CHALLENGES FOR EDUCATIONAL RESEARCH – ISBN 92-64-10030-X – © OECD 2003

OECD PUBLICATIONS, 2, rue André-Pascal, 75775 PARIS CEDEX 16
PRINTED IN FRANCE
(96 2003 03 1 P) ISBN 92-64-10030-X – No. 53029 2003